'ARE YOU LONESOME TONIGHT?'

ALAN BLEASDALE

faber and faber

LONDON · BOSTON

First published in 1985
by Faber and Faber Limited
3 Queen Square London WC1N 3AU

Filmset by Wilmaset Birkenhead Merseyside
Printed in Great Britain by
Whitstable Litho Ltd
Whitstable Kent
All rights reserved

British Library Cataloguing in Publication Data

Bleasdale, Alan
Are you lonesome tonight?
I. Title
822'.914   PS3552.L4/
ISBN 0–571–13732–6

Library of Congress Cataloging in Publication Data

Bleasdale, Alan
Are you lonesome tonight?
1. Presley, Elvis, 1935–1977—Drama.   I. Title.
PR6052.L397A89   1985   822'.914   85–6988
ISBN 0–571–13732–6 (pbk.)

The pure products of America go crazy.

William Carlos Williams (1883–1963)

They said I was all fucked up. I'm not fucked up by no means. On the contrary, I've never been in better condition in my life. I got a daughter and a life. I love to sing. After all, what profiteth a man if he gains the world and loses his own soul?

Elvis Presley, the year he died

ACKNOWLEDGEMENTS

For permission to reproduce the songs used in the script the publishers acknowledge the following with gratitude:

Belwin-Mills Music Ltd. for 'Heartbreak Hotel'; Carlin Music Corporation for 'Lawdy Miss Clawdy', 'I Want You, I Need You, I Love You', 'Don't Be Cruel', 'There's Good Rocking Tonight', 'If I Can Dream', 'All Shook Up', 'You Gave Me a Mountain This Time', 'I Was the One', 'Trying To Get To You' and 'Treat Me Nice'; Chappell Morris for 'Hound Dog'; Chappell Music Ltd. for 'Peace in the Valley'; Chappell Music Ltd. and Acuff Rose Music Ltd. for 'All My Trials, Lord'; Famous Chappell for 'I Don't Care if the Sun Don't Shine'; Redwood Music Ltd. for 'Are You Lonesome Tonight?'; Southern Music Publishing Co. Ltd., 8 Denmark St., London WC2H 8LT for 'Just Because'; and United Partnership for 'One Night'.

We would like to apologize for any errors or omissions in this list of acknowledgements.

A play is a team game. Otherwise, go away and write a novel. All playwrights, however, have different ways of getting through the process that finally produces the sheer terror of an opening. Personally, once the first draft is finished I send the script to those people, often of very different perspectives, who I have come to trust in their critical judgement of my work.

The list gets longer with every passing production, but I am glad to have this opportunity to thank the following friends for suffering my original naked, muddled, four-hour version of *Are You Lonesome Tonight?* – Caroline Smith, Michael Attenborough, Richard Brandon, Bill Morrison, Andrew Schofield, Michael Wearing, Bernard Hill, Elvis Costello, Bill Kenwright and Harvey Unna. The proofs of this edition were also corrected and cared for by Trevor Dann.

I write these notes some weeks before *Are You Lonesome Tonight?* goes into rehearsal. The usual fear is mixed with considerable optimism, because I know I am going to be working with an excellent director in Robin Lefevre, and a cast led by one of the bravest and best actors of his generation, Martin Shaw. This morning I saw a model for a tremendous set by Voytek, and Bill Kenwright is producing the play with regard for me and, much more importantly, love for that real working-class hero, man of charm, charisma, generosity of spirit, and sadly, perhaps in the final summing up, someone not quite conceited, unpleasant and knowing enough to survive. I also suspect that some will consider this play some kind of insult to Elvis Presley. I know enough to know that they are wrong. This is one from the heart.

Are You Lonesome Tonight? is dedicated to Bill Morrison, Timothy Bleasdale and Jo Beddoe. They all know why.

ALAN BLEASDALE
11.3.85

'*Are You Lonesome Tonight?*' was first performed at the Liverpool Playhouse on 14 May 1985. The cast included:

OLDER PRESLEY	Martin Shaw
YOUNGER PRESLEY	Simon Bowman
JO JO	Paul Ridley
REDHEAD	Colette Stevenson
MARTY	Michael Keating
DUKE	Peter Marinker
ENGLISHMAN	Robert East
GERRY	Ray Jewers
MARIE-ANNE	Stacey Hughes
GLADYS PRESLEY	Delia Lindsey
VERNON PRESLEY	Neville Whiting
COLONEL PARKER	Roger Booth
JEWELLER	Douglas Illes
PRISCILLA PRESLEY	Nancy Wood

Also prominently featured:
Julian Ashton, Jonathan Evans and Clyde Gatell

Director	Robin Lefevre
Designer	Voytek
Musical Director	Rod Edwards

PROLOGUE

Gracelands. Shrouded, like white ghosts.
We see and hear a funeral cortège crossing the stage. They are singing
'Peace in the Valley'. Not maudlin and morbid. Principal voice –
Black Female.

PRINCIPAL SINGER:
> Oh well, I'm so tired and so weary,
> But I must go along
> Till the Lord comes and calls,
> Calls me away, oh yes.
>
> Well, the morning so bright,
> And the lamp is alight,
> And the night is as black as a sea, oh yeah.
>
> There will be peace in the valley for me someday,
> There will be peace in the valley for me, oh Lord, I pray,
> There'll be no sadness, no sorrow, no trouble, trouble I
>   see,
> There will be peace in the valley for me.

(*At the back of the cortège, slightly distanced, is* COLONEL
PARKER *with a tray of relics and souvenirs, a stetson and a
ten-dollar bill.*)

COLONEL: Roll up, roll up . . .
(*He stands upstage centre as the cortège leaves the stage. He
takes off his tray. Takes out a bargepole of a cigar. Lights it.
Keeps the light going. Extends his arm, giving a flickering light
to the shrouded areas. Smiles. Blows out the light. Then, from
the folds in one of the shrouds, we hear and then see an Al
Jolson version of 'Are You Lonesome Tonight?' – with all its
racial grotesqueness of Sambo and shine.*)

AL JOLSON:
> Are you lonesome tonight,
> Do you miss me tonight,
> Are you sorry we drifted apart?

(He goes down on one knee and freezes. From another shrouded area, we hear and see a 1940s Sinatra/Johnny Ray type of tuberculosis sex appeal, with a sob in the throat.)

TB VICTIM:

Does your memory stray

To a bright summer day,

When I kissed you and called you sweetheart?

(And into freeze. To be followed, slipping out from another shrouded area, by the sound and sight of Country. And Western. Violins and Hank Williams.)

HANK:

Do the chairs in your parlour

Seem empty and bare,

Do you gaze at your doorstep and picture me there?

(The COLONEL *studies each performance behind a swirl of cigar smoke. And the* COUNTRY SINGER *gets three extra lines. While, in a place not yet clearly defined, beneath a cockerel logo, throbbing red, off and on perhaps, a* WHITE MAN *in his mid-thirties listens to the sound.)*

Is your heart filled with pain,

Shall I come back again,

Tell me dear, are you lonesome tonight?

(And the MAN *beneath the cockerel logo uses the words Presley used at the start of 'Milk Cow Blues' on one of his first 'Sun Sessions' . . .)*

SAM PHILIPS: Hold it fellers – that don't *move* me. Let's get real real gone for a change!

(Immediately we hear a sensual, almost rocking blues version of 'Are You Lonesome Tonight?' During the instrumental start, we see a WHITE BOY *and a* BLACK GIRL *jitterbug and jive all around and all over each other. Splendidly. And somewhere in the deep shadows of the scene and the space, back turned, dressed like a gaudy young hood, moving mild but loose to the music, and combing his quiff too, we might just catch the barest glimpse of the* YOUNGER PRESLEY. *And he will come closer to the* COUPLE *as they really begin to move. But he is still barely a silhouette. Simultaneous with the start of the rocking blues version of 'Are You Lonesome Tonight?' a white red-hot red-*

neck RACIST *arrives on stage, flat-footed and fat, an overhanging forehead, hat and overalls. He spews out his filth to the musical and highly physical background of the dancing and the rocking blues. He stands by a sign proclaiming* WE SERVE WHITE CUSTOMERS ONLY.)

RACIST: I am, and I tell you proudly, I am the Chairman of the Alabama White Citizens' Christian Council, and you see before you an Aryan man, yes an Aryan man, one Caucasian, no chains ever held me down, boy, I ain't never been in no treetops, I never ever been able to touch my toes without bending down, there's nothing wrong with my lips, and let me say here and now in this year of the Lord, 1954, screw the communists, there ain't no communists in Alabama, but them niggahs, man . . . (*Steps up a gear. Pop-eyed and shaking.*) No niggah comes in here for no gasoline, no niggah allowed in no automobile within this service station, not even as a white man's chauffeur, I don't even care if he comes in here with a rope around his neck pullin' the goddam car; and in addition I want you to know that I do not allow upon my premises, or in the sanctity of my God-fearin' home, none of that new-fangled, vulgar, animalistic niggah jive-arse rock an' roll bop! (*Half turns away, turns back.*) An' furthermore, they ain't got big dicks! (*As the* BLACK GIRL *moves towards a microphone, she continues to cut wild, loose and in celebration.*)

BLACK SINGER:
Do you gaze at your doorstep and picture me there?
Is your heart filled with pain,
Shall I come back again,
Tell me, dear, are you lonesome tonight?
(*As the final 'lonesome' version finishes, and as the lights go down on the* BLACK SINGER AND DANCER, *we see* SAM PHILIPS, *the desk and the chair. Sun Records. The logo of the cockerel at a red dawn.*)

SAM PHILIPS: . . . if I could find a White boy . . . hey no listen, if I could find me a White boy who had the Negro sound and the Negro feel, I could make myself a billion dollars. (*He laughs quietly to himself. And the* CARNIVAL

MAN *snorts contemptuously*.)

COLONEL: That's what you think, son! Come on, I know you're out there somewhere . . . but *where?*

(*In the spotlight, in the area used by the Black couple previously, we see the young bareboned* PRESLEY, *using a 1950s style microphone for all it is worth, as he batters his way into and through 'Lawdy Miss Clawdy'*.)

YOUNGER PRESLEY:

> Well, Lawdy Lawdy Lawdy Miss Clawdy,
> Gal, you sure look good to me,
> Well, please don't excite me, baby,
> I know it can't be me!
>
> I'd give you all my money,
> Yeah, but you just won't treat me right,
> You like to ball every mornin',
> Don't come home till late at night.
>
> Gonna tell, tell my mamma,
> Lord, I swear girl, what you've been doin' to me,
> I'm gonna tell everybody,
> That I'm down in misery.
>
> So bye, bye bye, baby,
> Gal, I won't be comin' no more,
> Goodbye little darlin',
> Down the road I go.

(*He finishes, laughing, happy, warm. The* COLONEL *is close by. He will begin to move* ELVIS *to a higher position. He is holding a white sports coat – the coat of a hoodlum.*)

COLONEL: That's my boy!

(*The other* SINGERS *turn away, and disappear and dissolve behind the folds of the shrouds. A glimpse of a couch in a living room. The red-necked* RACIST. *Slumped on a couch. His* WIFE *at his side. A* DOCTOR *standing over the* RACIST. *Stethoscope in hand.*)

WIFE: Well, doctor, he was sittin' there in front of the television dozing off, and it sort of got to the part of the song where the boy moved his body like he did, and Wilbur woke up, stood up, went a funny colour, held his chest, said, 'What's happenin' to America, that's a White boy!' – and kinda . . . died. Doctor.

(*We see the* YOUNGER PRESLEY *again, in another place, another spotlight, perhaps now wearing a hoodlum's white sports coat given to him by the* COLONEL. *He is looking moody and mean. He sings 'Heartbreak Hotel'.*)

YOUNGER PRESLEY:

> Well, since my baby left me, well I've found a new place to dwell,
> Well, it's down at the end of Lonely Street, that's Heartbreak Hotel
> Where I'll be; I'll make you so lonely, baby,
> Well, I'm so lonely, I'll be so lonely, I could die.
>
> Although it's always crowded, you still can find some room
> For broken-hearted lovers to cry there in the gloom,
> And I'll be so, I'll make you so lonely, baby,
> I'll make you so lonely, they're so lonely, they could die.
>
> Now the bell hop's tears keep flowing,
> The desk clerk's dressed in black,
> Well, they've been so long on Lonely Street
> They'll never never look back,
> And they'll be, they'll make you so lonely, baby, they're so lonely
> They're so lonely, they could die.

(*The* YOUNGER PRESLEY *changes tempo as he almost repeats the last few lines – with a quiet cold chill.*)

> Now this poor boy's tears keep flowing,
> They're waitin' to dress me in black,
> Well, I've been so long on Lonely Street
> I can never never look back,
> And I'll be, I'll make you so lonely, baby, I'm so lonely,
> Well, I'm so lonely, I could die.

(*The* YOUNGER PRESLEY *ends up in silhouette and frozen too.*)

ACT ONE

The white shrouds are flown away as we cross-fade into Gracelands. We see a film screen on the back wall. The film reel has broken. We hear the clicking sound of the same piece of film flicking through the projector as we see the image on the screen. And we see Gracelands, still in some darkness, coming to life. A round table, downstage centre. On the table will be a machine-gun, a guitar and a doctor's-type attaché case. Towels, dead food and drink. Debris. Telephones. Two aircraft-type chairs at the table have equal importance. One faces out. The other has been turned around to face the screen. Three other chairs of less glory are at the table.
Enter MARTY, REDHEAD *and* JO JO. MARTY *looks towards the screen. Goes to one of the phones. Phones. Waits impatiently.*

MARTY: Sam, f'Chrissake man, the film's snapped . . . yeah yeah, haven't we all.
  (*He puts down the phone. Quietly. The screen goes blank as 'Sam' brings the lights up in the room.* MARTY, JO JO *and* REDHEAD *are tip-toeing about, preparing for the Older Presley. And the* OLDER PRESLEY *turns slowly around in the big aircraft chair. He looks a lot better than he has any right to look. Looks around at them. Smiles slyly. Glances at his watch.*)

OLDER PRESLEY: Mornin'.
REDHEAD: Good mornin', honey.
  (MARTY *and* JO JO *look at each other.* MARTY *bites on the bullet.*)
MARTY: Well, er, would be, El, 'cept it's nine thirty; in the evenin'.
OLDER PRESLEY: Oh . . . Sure feels like mornin'.
NEARLY ALL OF THEM: Yeah!
REDHEAD: . . . Yeah!
  (*They busy themselves, perhaps getting a milk drink for* PRESLEY, *starting to clear the mess off the table, starting to*

14

relax. The phone rings. They all look towards the phone.
Nobody wants the honour.)

MARTY: There they go again, Boss.

OLDER PRESLEY: You worry too much, Marty.

(PRESLEY *flicks his fingers at* MARTY *and points to the phone*
on the table. Then he reaches for the inbuilt phone in his chair.
MARTY *and* PRESLEY *pick up a phone each – simultaneously.*
PRESLEY *listens. Silent – for the time being. And we also see a*
room above and to the side. Images of Old Southern
chandeliers, drapes, a feeling of a squalid past, present and
future, dark, dingy, cobwebby, hired by the night to fuck
someone. A table, three chairs, a phone and tape facilities.
DUKE, GERRY *and an* ENGLISHMAN *with a portable tape*
recorder. DUKE *is on the phone.*)

MARTY: Yeah?

DUKE: Duke.

MARTY: So?

DUKE: Just a talk, man, that's all. A talk with the man.

MARTY: Been told you're talkin' into a tape recorder these days,
Duke.

DUKE: (*Glancing at the others*) Just collectin' together some
memories, 's all.

MARTY: What d'you need the Boss for then? You make your
own memories. And your own lies.

DUKE: We just wanna clear a few things up. Get the truth.

OLDER PRESLEY: (*Joining in*) Not what I heard. Heard you
were plannin' a book.

DUKE: Hi Boss, thought you might be there somewhere.

OLDER PRESLEY: You bet – but about this book –

DUKE: It's a possibility. Gotta pay the bills.

OLDER PRESLEY: Yeah man, an' how far does thirty pieces of
silver go, these days?

DUKE: You started this –

OLDER PRESLEY: *An' I'm finishin' it.* There's only one name for
you now, the only name I'd recognize you by – Judas.
That's you, man. Judas.

DUKE: (*Evenly*) Yeah, you havin' supper in there or what?

OLDER PRESLEY: Just crawl off, Judas – but keep writin' that

15

book an' you're goin' nowhere, not even crawlin'. I'll see to that.

DUKE: You threatenin' me?

OLDER PRESLEY: Not as much as you're threatenin' me, Duke.

DUKE: Got the name wrong there, haven't you?

OLDER PRESLEY: (*Quietly*) Just go away. Next time I wanna see you is on your knees, Duke. Judas.

(PRESLEY *slams the phone down, so does* MARTY. *The lights fade down on* DUKE, GERRY *and the* ENGLISHMAN *as the phone is put down and the tape is turned off.*)

You heard them, Marty – they're doin' a book – an' I'll be bleedin' all over the bookstands of America . . . Good value for one dollar ninety-five . . . *Lies*. Even the truth'll be lies in their hands . . . What was I doin'? Before they called?

REDHEAD: You were sleepin', baby.

OLDER PRESLEY: They don't know – not even those two – not even Duke – I know that he's got – (*To* MARTY *and* JO JO) you know what he's got – but what he hasn't got is any idea what it's like to be me. Nobody knows. Nobody knows the truth. The whole truth and nothing but the truth. So help me, God. (*Laughs. Looks to the others, shrugs.*) Help me . . . You want the truth – I'll tell you the truth. Right from the start. (*Looks to* REDHEAD.) This time I'll be brave.

REDHEAD: But Elvis honey, some bits you can't face –

OLDER PRESLEY: No, this time. I'll get through it. Cos nobody knows. But me. Gonna have to face up to their version soon enough – may as well face my own. Mine has to be better than theirs. (*Laughs a little.*) I don't hate myself that much . . . I wanna see myself. Like I was. Like it was. Start again.

(*He turns away and points at the screen, as the lights fade down on them. We see* DUKE, GERRY *and the* ENGLISHMAN. *The* ENGLISHMAN *is testing his portable tape recorder. Perhaps all three are smoking.*)

ENGLISHMAN: One two, one two –

DUKE: But what's it worth? *What is it worth?*

ENGLISHMAN: Depends on what you have on him – and if you can prove it.

16

DUKE: I can prove it all right. If I want to.

ENGLISHMAN: If you want to?

DUKE: (*Shrugs.*) Depends on how far we have to go. If we wanna go that far. If it's worth it. But I have got something – and you won't believe what I have got.

ENGLISHMAN: I'll believe it. If you've got it.

DUKE: *But what's it worth?*

ENGLISHMAN: How do I know – till you tell me.

DUKE: If I tell you.

ENGLISHMAN: All right. Just tell me the story.

DUKE: (*Laughs.*) Saddest story you'll ever hear.

ENGLISHMAN: Well, let's hear it then. From the start.

(*He clicks the tape recorder on. The lights slowly fade down on them.*)

DUKE: Y'know about Jesse?

ENGLISHMAN: . . . Jesse James?

(*Laughter from* DUKE *and* GERRY. *We see, at first, what appears to be a still frame:* VERNON *and* GLADYS *and* ELVIS PRESLEY – *like The Grapes of Wrath.* GLADYS *in a cheap patterned dress.* VERNON *wearing a faded shirt, a hat tipped back on his head. Both look handsome and young, but already grim and tired. All three are looking away from the camera to their left as if expecting something miserable to happen.* ELVIS *is 3 years old, a sharecropper's kid in dungarees and a two-tone shirt too short in the arms. With a hat very dissimilar to his father's, the brim at an almost rakish angle over his right eye. And a curled lip. They sit silent, staring out to their left. And we hear the instrumental start of the traditional song, 'All My Trials, Lord', as an* OFFICER OF THE LAW *arrives within the 'frame' of the picture from the direction they have been looking anxiously towards. He laconically handcuffs* VERNON PRESLEY. *Departs with him.* MOTHER *and* CHILD *stay mute and still, except that their eyes follow the departing* OFFICER *and* VERNON *as they move across the stage.*)

PRINCIPAL SINGER:
> If living were a thing that money could buy,
> You know the rich would live and the poor would die,
> All my trials, Lord, soon be over.

(GLADYS PRESLEY *joins in the second verse*.)

BOTH WOMEN:

> Hush little baby, don't you cry,
> You know your mama was born to die,
> All my trials, Lord, soon be over.

(*And the* BOY PRESLEY *grips hold of her. She huddles him around her. Mother and child – that's all.*)

GLADYS PRESLEY: Hey hey, hush now, it'll be all right, Elvis. Least I still got you an' Jesse, son. Yes, two fine boys . . .

(*We see* DUKE, GERRY *and the* ENGLISHMAN.)

DUKE: How would you handle it, man? With a ghost in the closet, and every day of your life, your mama sets a table for four.

GERRY: When there's only three at the table.

DUKE: Providing his daddy wasn't in jail.

ENGLISHMAN: His mother . . . ?

GERRY: He loved her twice as much as any son could.

DUKE: He had to. He was givin' her Jesse's love as well.

ENGLISHMAN: So his mother never accepted –

DUKE: *He* never accepted. Jesse's as real to him as you are to me.

ENGLISHMAN: When . . . when did you first meet him?

DUKE: The first time? I came to his rescue the first time. You know. Like your Robin Hood. With Maid Marian.

(*He laughs as the lights fade down on them.*)

A soda fountain. 1953.

The YOUNGER PRESLEY, *back almost turned. Moving, combing his hair in the reflection from the chrome of a juke-box. He kicks the juke-box. Instrumental music begins to play: 'Just Because'.*

YOUNGER PRESLEY *starts whistling and then singing. His body movements get bigger. He watches himself. But does not see* TWO YOUNG THUGS *as they approach from the side. They watch the performance until they can no longer contain their giggling hatred.*

YOUNGER PRESLEY:

> Well well well just because you think you're so pretty,
> And just because your mama thinks you're hot,
> Well, just because you think you've got something that

18

        no other girl's got,
    You cause me to spend all my money, you laughed and –
    (*The* TWO THUGS *laugh.* PRESLEY *turns to face them, but still*
    hardly able to keep still. One THUG *pushes him hard in the*
    chest.)
THUG A: What's up with you, boy?
THUG B: An' friggin' well keep still when we're talkin' to you –
    wormin' around like some kind of niggah.
THUG A: Or some kind of friggin' faggot. (*Brushes his hand hard*
    against PRESLEY'*s cheek.*) You wearin' make-up? You are!
    Been told – mascara – you wear mascara!
    (*He knocks* PRESLEY *hard against the juke-box. The music*
    whines down to a stop.)
YOUNGER PRESLEY: Hell, no, I just got dark eyes –
THUG A: Mama's boy, is that what you is?
    (PRESLEY *goes still immediately and then raises a fist. The fist*
    is caught by ONE *of the two* THUGS. *The* OTHER ONE *goes to*
    hit PRESLEY *and then stops as we see a fourth person step from*
    out of the shadows with a billiard cue: DUKE.)
DUKE: Beat it, assholes . . . I said beat it – or eat this.
    (*He indicates the billiard cue.*)
THUG A: Sure, Duke . . .
    (*The* TWO THUGS *slide off.* PRESLEY *faces* DUKE.)
DUKE: Assholes. (*Looks towards* PRESLEY. *Looks him up and*
    down.) Wanna know somethin' – the whole world's full of
    assholes. You name them – they're assholes.
YOUNGER PRESLEY: Yeah?
DUKE: Yeah. Everybody's an asshole.
YOUNGER PRESLEY: (*Laughs nervously.*) What does that make
    me?
DUKE: (*Flatly*) A different kind of asshole.
    (*He walks away, leaving* PRESLEY *alone, staring after him.*
    Slowly, without being aware, PRESLEY *starts moving to the*
    music again as he takes his comb out and plays with his quiff
    and begins once again to whistle. Then kicks the juke-box and
    the song begins again.)
YOUNGER PRESLEY:
    Well well well, just because you think you're so pretty,

And just because your mama thinks you're the hottest
thing in town . . .
(*He starts laughing, mockingly. Points to the chrome 'mirror'.
Weighs himself up very carefully.*)
Asshole.

Back at Gracelands.
OLDER PRESLEY: Twenty-four years. Down the can . . .
(*He tries to laugh, barely succeeds. The phone rings.* JO JO
answers it.)
JO JO: Yeah yeah, send him up, Charlie. (*Puts the phone down.*)
That's –
OLDER PRESLEY: Must be gettin' old, I'm countin' the years,
but that's how long we go back, honey, me an' those two,
particularly Duke. (*Shakes his head.*) *Duke.*
JO JO: That new jeweller you wanted to –
OLDER PRESLEY: It is, it's gonna crucify me, that book, an' it's
not fair – it's nowhere near Good Friday . . . They can't do
this to me . . . (*Very quietly*) Can they?
JO JO: Nah. *Nah.* Not you. Not the King, man.
OLDER PRESLEY: Kings. And Dukes. And Queens. An' Duke's
got checkmate on my Queen. My former Queen. An' if he
uses it, the game is over. And the King is dead. But he
wouldn't use it . . . would he?
REDHEAD: Course not, honey.
(*She hasn't got a clue what he is talking about.* The
JEWELLER *enters – very nervously – with jewellery case, a
large ring on his finger, smiling sickeningly.*)
JEWELLER: I'm very honour–
OLDER PRESLEY: Yeah yeah, sit down.
(*The* JEWELLER *goes to sit down on the 'throne' next to*
PRESLEY.)
Not there. No one sits there.
(*The* JEWELLER *throws himself into the next seat along, opens
his case and pops up a display tray of all that glitters. And is
gold. And carats. Rings mainly.* PRESLEY *stares out, not
looking at him or the jewellery.*)
(*Finally*) I need somethin' – wish I knew what it was –
what do I need?

(*He looks to* REDHEAD, *then the* JEWELLER, MARTY *and* JO
JO. JEWELLER *moves his tray that bit nearer, smiling all the
way.*)
Give me 'fifty-eight.
(*The* JEWELLER *looks at his tray. The* OTHERS *look away.*)
Tell you what, give me 'fifty-six first.
(*The* JEWELLER *is trying to count without being obvious.*)
(*Into the phone*) Come on, Marie Anne. (*To the* OTHERS)
Give me 'fifty-six. And give me the truth.
JEWELLER: I can truthfully say that this collection represents –
(PRESLEY *looks at the* JEWELLER, *looks to the* OTHERS,
grins, then speaks into the phone. As he does so, JO JO *leans
across to the* JEWELLER, *shakes his head, puts his finger to his
mouth, mimes silence.*)
OLDER PRESLEY: Marie-Anne, breakfast beautiful, big baby,
just like your good self . . . What? Oh I dunno . . . (*looks
around.*) Four portions of hashed browns, coupla pound of
bacon, a lot of that gravy, two of sauerkraut, some crowder
peas and a whole stack of fried tomatoes – oh an' five or six
eggs. (*Looks around again.*) Any of you want anythin'?
(*They all shake their heads.*)
Lots of gravy, Marie-Anne, gotta look after myself – (*grins,
looks at the others*) – while I'm lookin' at myself. (*Puts the
phone down.*) I wanna see myself. And I wanna see my
mama. See it all. Colonel Parker too. Yeah!
(*Nobody can look at him, however happy he seems.*)
REDHEAD: Baby, honey baby, you know it makes you unhappy.
And we've got the latest Robert Redford movie.
OLDER PRESLEY: You're kiddin' me aren't y' – Robert
Redford? You seen those warts – face like a mountain
range – more warts than the Wicked Witch! An' that's the
truth.
(*He laughs. They laugh. He stops. They stop.*)
Truth – huh – what do they know about the truth – that
pair of Judases? (*Points.*) *Get some pictures on that screen.*
REDHEAD: (*Trying to whisper*) You'll cry.
OLDER PRESLEY: I won't, I'll make sure of that. Where's my
friend, where's my best friend, where's my doctor man?

(*Looks to* MARTY *and* JO JO.) Take care of business – that's
what you're here for – now do it.

(*He sees* REDHEAD *looking disapproving, throws himself into a
song as* MARTY *and* JO JO *exchange glances and* MARTY *goes
off. He struggles to his feet, laughing at himself.*)

    I'm going to hold my baby as tight as I can,
    Well, tonight she'll know I'm a mighty mighty man,
    I heard the news, there's good rockin' tonight!

(*He swivels his hips, grins at her, ignores the* JEWELLER.)

REDHEAD: (*Not ignoring the* JEWELLER) You don't need this,
honey. There's some parts that always make you –

OLDER PRESLEY: I'll close my eyes. (*Misses a beat, and then
turns on* JO JO.) *Find the man and get him to put the goddam
thing back on.*

(*Silence.* JO JO *stares at him mournfully.*)

I mean, what d'you buy dogs for? Hey? *Hey?*

(JO JO *looks bleakly at him, then walks away.* PRESLEY *half
stumbles a few paces after him.*)

You gonna write a book about me? You too, Jo Jo? Joinin'
the others? (*Turns on* REDHEAD.) How about you, hon?

(*Doesn't get a reply, turns back towards where* JO JO *has gone.*)
'The Truth about Elvis' – the mother likes big breakfasts!
Bought me a fine big house an' a showroom full of cars –
one bad bad mother – the people of America should be
told! . . . I'm sorry, Jo Jo, I'm . . . sor–

(*He motions an apology with his hands. But* JO JO *has gone.*
PRESLEY *moves back towards his seat. Puts his hands
affectionately and genuinely on* REDHEAD's *shoulders as he
stands behind her. She puts her hands on his.*)

I didn't mean . . . you know that, Red. Just . . . the dogs
are barkin' all right. They're barkin' back. And behind my
back. After all I've done, all the things I know are *good*, and
. . . Anyway . . . how is my dog, honey?

(*He smiles down at her. She looks away and winces.*)

What's the news? (*Sits down.*) That old boy, Getlo, I sure
miss him.

REDHEAD: (*Slightly nervously*) Well, they er, the hospital sort of
said something about the blood picture being pretty bad,

honey, and you know how high his blood pressure was, but the er surgeon said they're thinkin' about – (*glances at him*) – a kidney transplant, dialysis maybe.

OLDER PRESLEY: Whatever. Tell them – whatever – the money doesn't matter. Get him fixed – I want him here. By my side. It's been a long time an' one thing for certain, he won't be sellin' his story. (*Laughs. Becomes a reporter:*) 'What was it like bein' Elvis Presley's dog, son?'
(*He barks and growls. Both of them end up laughing.*)
I'm just . . . I'm upset, 's all, but bein' upset's enough . . . (*To* JEWELLER *who was beginning to think he was invisible*) Don't you think?

JEWELLER: Well sure, Mr Presley.

OLDER PRESLEY: My friends call me 'Elvis'.

JEWELLER: Ah right. Elvis.

OLDER PRESLEY: You can call me 'Mr Presley' . . . (*Finally grins, leans across and puts his hand easily on the* JEWELLER's *arm.*) You were sayin' about bein' upset.

JEWELLER: Er . . . well, everyone has a right to be : . . upset. I get upset.
(PRESLEY *raises his eyebrows in mock surprise.*)
Sometimes.

OLDER PRESLEY: Sure you do. But cos it's me that's upset, it's worse – you don't believe that, do you?

JEWELLER: (*In panic*) Well, I er, you're kinda –
(*He points desperately towards the heavens.*)

OLDER PRESLEY: I'm in the attic?
(*He too looks up.*)

JEWELLER: No – for you, bein' who you are, it must –

OLDER PRESLEY: (*Flatly*) I'm the King. (*Then almost as an aside to the* JEWELLER) I'll take the works, man, the whole works, I'll take every last mother.

JEWELLER: That's wond – that's – but that's a lot of money –

OLDER PRESLEY: And I'll take the ring on your finger. I'll even take the finger. Name the price. *Name the price.*

JEWELLER: Ah, come on, Elv– Mr Presley – I mean, this is just . . . a pleasure to me. I don't –

OLDER PRESLEY: A lady said that once to me – then tried to

sell her story to the *National Enquirer* . . . (*Gently*) All
right, just tell me the cost of all that pleasure. That's all.
(MARTY *returns as the* JEWELLER *begins to count – in
thousands – silently, with a pocket calculator.*)

MARTY: The doc's on his way, boss, but he said you got
enough. (*Quickly*) He's still comin' though.

OLDER PRESLEY: You bet he is. An' I ain't got enough. Cos
I've had enough. And if I've had enough, I ain't got
enough . . .
(JO JO *returns, doesn't look at* PRESLEY, *deliberately sits
down, facing out, despite* PRESLEY *looking at him.* PRESLEY
turns on the JEWELLER, *puts his hand on the calculator.*)
Count outside. (*Laughs.*) Hey, we got a real live Count with
us! Count Outside, brother of Count Dracula and Count the
Cost!
(*Everyone except* JO JO *laughs.*)
Hey, I feel good, I told you I would, come on.
(*He glances towards the sullen* JO JO, *reaches down and picks
up his guitar, goes towards* JO JO, *stops and turns back.*)
See Charlie, he'll sort it out.
(PRESLEY *flicks the jewellery tray shut.*)

JEWELLER: I'd just like to say –

OLDER PRESLEY: Goodbye. Yeah sure. Charlie's around. All
right? Have a nice day. Or night. Now. By the way, y'
won't get a book out of this, you know. Nah . . . (*Flashes
the warmest smile you ever did see. He turns away, looks
towards the glum* JO JO. *The* JEWELLER *goes out, hardly
believing this is happening.* PRESLEY *moves towards and then
behind* JO JO, *strapping his guitar on. He spins* JO JO'*s chair
around and throws himself into a deliberate caricature of Elvis
the Pelvis, singing 'I Want You, I Need You, I Love You':*)
Hold me close, hold me tight,
Make me thrill with delight,
Let me know where I stand from the start,
I want you, I need you, I love you with all my heart.
(REDHEAD *and* MARTY *join in the background vocals.
Finally, but only when* MARIE-ANNE, *the Black maid/cook
arrives during the second verse with Presley's monstrous*

24

breakfast on a huge tray, plus a litre of strawberry milkshake,
JO JO *cracks up.* MARIE-ANNE *puts the tray of food on the*
table to fester and joins in the singing with PRESLEY *and the*
OTHERS. JO JO *cracks up because* MARIE-ANNE *has an awful*
voice and little rhythm – and gets a solo on the third verse, at
PRESLEY's *nod.*)

MARIE-ANNE:
  Everytime that you're near,
  All my cares disappear,
  Jo Jo, you're all that I'm living for,
  I want you, I need you, I love you, more and more.

JO JO: All right, all right, I give in. Jesus Christ!

(PRESLEY *puts his arm around* MARIE-ANNE.)

OLDER PRESLEY: Marie-Anne, baby, you ain't been here long,
  but I tell y', darlin', y've already made a big impression on
  me – yeah – y' the only Black woman I know who sings
  just like Bob Dylan, an' moves with all the grace an'
  rhythm of President Ford.

(*Laughter. Genuine. No racist overtones at all – or undertones.*
MARIE-ANNE *laughs the loudest as she leaves, humming badly,*
as PRESLEY *sits down to his late evening breakfast and begins*
to devour, with fingers and fork, the food before him.)

Go an' see if Count Outside's still outside, Reds, an' bring
those pretty baubles back in here.

(REDHEAD *shimmies out, wonderfully and naturally.* JO JO
and MARTY *can't help looking at her as* PRESLEY *looks at*
them and eats savagely.)

Y' can look but y' better not touch . . . Hey, last night, last
night, fellers, feelin' horny, I said, 'Reds baby, tell y' what
– let's make love with the light on.' Know what she said –
'No way – an' shut the car door, f'Christ's sake!'

(*They all laugh, like good old boys, as the lights dim down on*
them. PRESLEY *looks away, shoulders sagging,*
whispering . . .)

I gotta face it . . . gotta do it tonight . . .

(*'Casually' he begins to pull the attaché case towards himself as*
the OTHERS *watch out of the corners of their eyes. He takes the*
attaché case, stands, walks towards the doors.)

(*Looking back*) Just got somethin' t' do first – it's all right.
(*He turns away, and straight into* REDHEAD *returning with jewels. He smiles and charms, she stays stone-faced.*)
I'll be all right.
(*He leaves. She glowers towards the table, sits down.*)
REDHEAD: Well, I think I'd like to see some warts.
MARTY: (*Into intercom*) Run the Redford, Sammy.

DUKE *and* GERRY *and the* ENGLISHMAN.
DUKE *is banging on the table with his fingers – a very strong finger.*
DUKE: . . . cos those selfsame drugs that are killin' Elvis were killin' us as well.
GERRY: You had to take them. If you were there, you had to take them too.
DUKE: Generous to a fault, that was Elvis.
ENGLISHMAN: What – (*Hears a click, glances down at his tape recorder, sees he has to turn the tape over, talks as he does so.*) You must really . . . hate him. (*Looks up.*) *Now*. After what –
DUKE: (*Violently*) Got every right to – and so what – what's it to you?
(*Silence. The* ENGLISHMAN *looks away.*)
And anyway, you know where hate comes from? (*Prods the* ENGLISHMAN *in the chest.*) From the heart. Where love is found. (*Laughs. Looks to* GERRY.) Sounds like a country song.
(*They both smile – until* DUKE *jabs the* ENGLISHMAN *again.*)
And what've you got there – got anythin' there – or anywhere?
(*Embarrassed silence. The* ENGLISHMAN *clicks on the tape.*)
ENGLISHMAN: What . . . what sort of drugs?
DUKE: (*Sardonically*) Every sort – but how we doin' so far? What's it worth? Hmmm? (*Leans forward.*) In dollars and cents . . .
ENGLISHMAN: If . . . if you could name . . . what he was taking . . .
DUKE: Biphetamines, Dexedrine, Amytal, Percodans, Qualudes by the handful, Diaudids – likes them a lot, Elvis does, eats

26

them up in private – Valium, Valmid, Nembutals, Phenobarbs –

GERRY: And that was just for breakfast.

ENGLISHMAN: Look, with the greatest respect, all this has to be . . . proved.

(DUKE *and* GERRY *nod cheerfully*.)

But it would – it would kill him.

DUKE: (*Shrugs.*) Ain't dead yet.

ENGLISHMAN: But why?

DUKE: (*With surprising quiet regret*) Well . . . what do you give a man who's got everything? All you can give him is more. And more. And more. Until one day . . . he can't take any more.

GERRY: Well? How we shapin' up?

DUKE: Coach.

ENGLISHMAN: It's not the picture . . . that's painted.

DUKE: It ain't a picture. It's a man. An' with a man, if you scratch the surface, you draw blood.

ENGLISHMAN: (*Shakes his head.*) You've done more than that – you've burst a boil – and the pus is there for all to see.

DUKE: What's the price like for pus?

(*As the lights fade down on them. We see the* OLDER PRESLEY *– alone at first, with guitar, playing a slower version of 'Don't Be Cruel'*.)

OLDER PRESLEY:

You know I can be found,
Sitting home all alone,
If you can't come around,
At least please telephone –

(*He sees little* LISA MARIE *watching him, puts his guitar down*)

I can see you, honey!

(*He approaches to pick her up in his arms in the most loving manner. He hugs her.*)

You been here long, Baby Bunting?

(*She nods her head gravely.*)

Like that song?

(*She nods.*)

Daddy just got to singing – like when you remember

27

someone who isn't here any more – happens as you get older – nothin' to worry about. (*Tickles her.*) Just yet. (*Grins.*) Hey, Bo Peep, you like bein' here with your daddy?
(*She nods.*)
You do anythin' else but nod?
(*She shakes her head. They both laugh.*)
Been a long time, sweetheart, I been away . . . been sick . . . come on, time passes too fast, come down and watch the movies with me. And the memories. (*Puts her down.*) Gettin' too heavy for an old old man . . . (*Kneels down to face her.*) Listen, angel, daddy's got somethin' to . . . you better know . . . you see, some people are gonna – people you probably seen hangin' around here once – huh – *once*, but bad things are gonna be said about me, darlin' – an' sure as eggs is eggs someone's gonna tell you – kids're like that – I know that – persecuted me at times – cos I was different – an' I was good – an' then when I was grown up because of who I am – but these things – they're not true – lies, sweetness – just jealous lies – don't you ever believe them, you hear?
(*She nods. He laughs and kisses her lightly.*)
And listen, you never be frightened of me, promise? Your mummy's a . . . good mummy, I know she'll never do that to you . . . but don't you ever be scared to come an' see me – be my friend – 'spite what anyone says . . . You know I love you, Snow White, don't you?
(*Again she nods gravely. Again he kisses her on the forehead. He stands with the slightest of difficulty. Everything seems warm and loving and what more could he want? Then he stoops down and picks up his plastic bag, hesitates, does not look at his daughter.*)
Just wait over there, babes, y' daddy's just got to . . . finish somethin'.
(*He walks one way, she walks the other.*)
He thought he'd finished . . . but he hasn't . . .
(*The lights fade down on the scene.*)

DUKE *and* GERRY *and the* ENGLISHMAN.
The whisky near gone. And the conversation.
DUKE: You know any of them Monty Python?
ENGLISHMAN: No, not really . . . I was in the same restaurant
    as John Cleese once.
GERRY: Oh yeah? What's he like?
ENGLISHMAN: Tall.
DUKE: His favourite film – *Monty Python and the Holy Grail.*
    Seen it five times in one night. Loved that bit where –
    (*The phone rings. All three jump a touch.* DUKE *goes to it.*)
ENGLISHMAN: Now you know –
DUKE: Yeah yeah.
ENGLISHMAN: Make sure you're recording –
DUKE: I know one thing, George Washington did us all a
    favour . . . (*Picks up the phone, presses the recording
    machine.*) Duke . . . I don't know what time I'll be back,
    Suzanne . . . Darlin', you eat – I'm here because I want us
    all to eat and drink and live in years to come. One night
    ain't gonna make no difference. (*Throws the phone down,
    looks at the others, begins to walk away from them.*) There's a
    liquor store open on the corner of Tenth . . . (*The lights
    begin to fade down on the remaining two.*)
GERRY: I was at a party once with the Beatles.
ENGLISHMAN: Oh. And what were *they* like?
GERRY: Dunno. The Boss wouldn't let us talk to them . . .

Gracelands.
The OLDER PRESLEY *enters with* LISA MARIE *in his arms. He also
has between his lips a party toy that blows raspberries. He lets* LISA
MARIE *slide out of his arms and run towards* REDHEAD. *She
snuggles in her arms as* PRESLEY *blows raspberries and approaches*
REDHEAD *and* LISA MARIE. *He opens the jewellery case for* LISA
MARIE.
OLDER PRESLEY: Close your eyes, sweetness. All right, open
    them now. Which one do you want? (*She selects.*) That one?
    . . . You've got good taste . . . expensive taste too.
    (*Then, without looking – because pride is involved –* PRESLEY
    slides the remnants of the jewellery case towards the two men.)

29

Take the rest – just a small . . . (*Holds his hands out in apology, still without looking*.) An' don't say thanks – I don't deserve no thanks – I been bad . . . to you. (*Shrugs. Blows a big raspberry, flings the toy away*.) I just can't help . . . Are we ready then? Come on! (*Looks around*.) 'Fifty-four. My first record, Lisa Marie. The summer of 'fifty-four, this old boy here was a young boy of 19 – and this is the day, darlin', here I am – stoppin' off at Sun Records – payin' my two dollars – singin' away – makin' a recordin' – for my mama's birthday – (*looks sideways at everbody*) – though really it was for me – couldn't wait to hear myself – standin' there waitin' – sweet voice of a woman on the Tannoy askin' for my address – said she liked my sound, Lisa Marie – *she liked my sound*! Sweet Jesus! (*Laughs*.) Liked it so much I was waitin' months . . . But then, then, here it is, angel – here it is!

(*He is carried away by his performance for her. All the others seem to be watching him. He is focused on* LISA MARIE. JO JO *then stands, leans across the table and slides the medical attaché case gently towards himself – knife and nerve edge. He will, as the scene progresses, slide the lock and lift the lid.* MARTY *and* REDHEAD *are sideways aware of his actions.* JO JO *begins frantically but quietly to take pills and boxes out of his pockets, as if he has been waiting for such a moment. His final move is to take what looks like a plastic toiletries bag from out of somewhere surrounding his body. He is about to exchange it for an identical bag in the attaché case when* PRESLEY *finally catches him. All he can do is drop the bag in his hands into the case.*)

. . . the day was nearly done, darlin', been drivin' my truck down the turnpike like my daddy did – comin' home to find a message from Mr Sam Philips of Sun Records – your darlin' grandmother was shakin' with excitement, big old eyes moist with tears, daddy there in the corner sulkin', callin' me a fag without once openin' his mouth, little Jesse's place still laid at the table . . . runnin' all those blocks, singin' like a high-pitched chicken headin' for the Sun, see me – *see me*, Baby Bunting!

(*He turns, sees* JO JO, *who just has time to drop the bag.*)
What y' doin'?

JO JO: Oh er, just takin' another er . . . (*Holds his head with one
hand, pushes the attaché case towards the centre of the table
with his other hand.*) Feelin' kind of . . .

OLDER PRESLEY: Sure – but don't take too many – stay in
control now, y' hear? But hey baby, it's all right, it's me,
look it's me, I'm really runnin', see me runnin', Mr Philips,
Mr Philips, I'm still runnin', that woman kept tellin' her
boss about this White boy with *that* voice, I'm comin', Mr
Philips, I'm a-comin'!

(*The* YOUNGER PRESLEY *bursts on. The* OLDER PRESLEY
and the others are facing out, across the table. The YOUNGER
PRESLEY *may make use of the table as he would a stage. He
batters into the start of 'There's Good Rocking Tonight'. And he
moves.*)

YOUNGER PRESLEY:

Well, I heard the news, there's good rockin' tonight,
Well, I heard the news, there's good rockin' tonight,
I'm gonna hold my baby as tight as I can,
Tonight she'll know I'm a mighty mighty man.
I heard the news, there's good rockin' tonight.

I said meet me in a hurry, behind the barn,
Don't you be afraid, that I'll do you no harm,
I want you to bring along my rockin' shoes,
Tonight I'm going to rock away all my blues,
I heard the news, there's good rockin' tonight.

Well, we're goin' to rock, we're going to rock, yes rock,
Come on an' rock, we're goin' to rock all our blues away.
Have you heard the news, everybody's rockin' tonight,
Have you heard the news, everybody's rockin' tonight.
I'm going to hold my baby as tight as I can.
Well, tonight she'll know I'm a mighty mighty man.
I heard the news, there's good rockin' tonight.

Well, we're goin' to rock, rock rock rock, come on an'
rock.

> Well, rock rock rock rock, well let's rock rock rock,
> We're goin' to rock all our blues away!
> (*As 'Good Rocking Tonight' comes to its frenzied finish,*
> PRESLEY *seems to go into freeze frame, and then the complete*
> *scene goes into darkness.*)

DUKE *and* GERRY *and the* ENGLISHMAN.

DUKE *laughing quietly as the lights fade up on them.*

DUKE: You've read too many fan magazines, son. Wasn't like
that at all. *An' I was there*. He sang like he had a frog in his
throat – or an elephant more like. Never seen no one so
nervous.

GERRY: Old Sam Philips put his arm around him . . . took him
to one side . . . and left him there.

ENGLISHMAN: So . . . ? How did – ?

DUKE: (*Easily*) He got lucky – Sam Philips went back to his
office, holdin' his nose, sittin' there tellin' his secretary she
don't know a good singin' voice from snake's piss – left the
tapes rollin' . . .
(*We see the* YOUNGER PRESLEY *in the recording studio, sitting*
on a stool, withdrawn, nervous. We hear, and perhaps see, the
BAND *as they goof and boogy through an introduction to 'I*
Don't Care if the Sun Don't Shine'. The YOUNGER PRESLEY
is isolated from them, but near the microphone. None of the
others playing can sing, and they miss the first opportunity for
the vocal. The YOUNGER PRESLEY *sings it to himself, looking*
around.)
Band started jammin' – an goofin' around – no one was
watchin' – Elvis began to relax . . .
(PRESLEY *hits the vocal section, second time around, to 'I*
Don't Care if the Sun Don't Shine', gaining in confidence as he
goes.)

YOUNGER PRESLEY:
> Well, I don't care if the sun don't shine,
> Get my lovin' in the evenin' time,
> When I'm with my baby
> Well, there ain't no fun with the sun around,
> I get goin' when the sun goes down,

And I'm with my baby.
Well, it's when we're going to kiss and kiss and kiss and
   kiss,
And kiss some more,
Who cares how many times we kiss,
At a time like this, who keeps score?
Well, I don't care if the sun don't shine,
I get my lovin' in the evenin' time,
When I'm with my baby.

Well, I don't care if the sun don't shine,
Get my lovin' in the evenin' time,
When I meet my baby.
And it don't matter if it's sleet or snow,
A drive-in's cosy when the lights are low,
And I'm with my baby.
Makes no difference if the rain comes down,
I don't notice when she's around.
Oh boy, what a baby.
Well, it's when we're going to kiss and kiss and kiss and
   kiss,
and we're gonna kiss some more.
Well, one kiss from my baby darlin' makes me holler –
'More, more more more!'
Well, I don't care if the sun don't shine,
I get my lovin' in the evenin' time,
When I meet my baby.

(*The* YOUNGER PRESLEY *finishes, looks around, sees* SAM
PHILIPS *approaching him ready to put his arm around him.*)

DUKE: An' Sam Philips was sat there in his office, hearin' that
   voice he'd been waitin' for. An' all it was was an accident.
   (*Grins.*)
GERRY: While the rest is history.
DUKE: But the other stuff is legend. Legend. Even the man
   himself believes it now. In fact, he started it . . .
ENGLISHMAN: But he was good. Wasn't he?
DUKE: Good? The boy was fucking amazing once he got going.
   (*The lights fade down on them.*)

The viewing room at Gracelands.

LISA MARIE *asleep in front of a sweating and exhausted* OLDER PRESLEY.

OLDER PRESLEY: She went asleep.

REDHEAD: It's late, way past her –

OLDER PRESLEY: But she went asleep. (*Pulls himself out of his childishness.*) Still, do I feel good. Yeah – gonna surprise you all before the night is out. They're lookin' for the truth – I'm gonna find it first . . .
    (*He has moved towards his attaché case. As casually as ever just puts his hand in and takes out the small plastic bag as the* OTHERS *watch.*)
    Takin' Sleepin' Beauty to bed – but I wanna see that handsome boy there when I come back – I tell y' – (*points out*) – that boy is goin' to be a star, I wouldn't be at all surprised if he isn't on that old Louisiana Hayride before too long . . .
    (*He picks* LISA MARIE *up, begins to move away, cradling her.*)

JO JO: I'll er come with you, Boss.

OLDER PRESLEY: (*Edge*) Put you to bed, too? You want nursery rhymes as well?
    (*He goes off: do not follow – or else. As soon as he goes off, the* OTHER THREE *dive at the attaché case.* JO JO *sticks his hand into the bag, takes his hand out, holding a plastic bag, opens it, throws a syringe on to the table and a sachet of white powder. Tastes it . . .*)

JO JO: Ah shit! Aspirin. He's got the goods . . .
    (REDHEAD *turns away and cries, genuinely, quietly.*)
    I'm leavin' here, man, I'm goin', it's too much. (*Looks up.*) I am not a baby sitter. Repeat – I am not a baby sitter.

REDHEAD: He's sick. He's not a baby.

JO JO: I didn't mean –

REDHEAD: And if he is, he's mine.

JO JO: You know what I meant.
    (MARTY *is already pulling other bottles of tablets from everywhere in his clothing.*)

MARTY: Yeah all right, y' mean well, the pair of y', but in the meantime . . .

34

(*He starts replacing roughly half of* PRESLEY's *'real' tablets with 'false' ones. The* OTHER TWO *frantically join in.* MARIE-ANNE *saunters in to collect the breakfast, looking out towards the 'screen' as she walks.*)

MARIE-ANNE: Is there ever anythin' on that screen?

JO JO: (*Not focusing on her*) Yeah sometimes – we got some of his early concerts . . . television shows . . . interviews . . .

MARIE-ANNE: But when there's nothin' there, there's like . . . nothin'? You only pretendin'?

JO JO: (*Mimicking*) 'Sright – we only pretendin'. (*Glances up.*) It makes the man happy.

MARIE-ANNE: But how do you do it, boys, sittin' here night after night, watchin' nothin' – starin' out at that blank screen . . . pretendin'?

JO JO: Sometimes he plays real movies an' sometimes he goes to sleep an' we play real movies. *All right?*
(*They continue changing the tablets as they talk.* MARIE-ANNE *lingers, listening, behind their backs.*)

REDHEAD: He's been askin' about Getlo again.

JO JO: Jesus, that dog – the friggin' thing's been dead two years.

MARTY: I told you y' should have told him there an' then.

REDHEAD: I couldn't –

MARTY: I mean, how much longer this gonna go on? The dog'll end up bein' fifty-nine years old an' still on some life-support system in a Los Angeles hospital. (*Imitates a very old* PRESLEY:) 'How's my dog doin', Hon? Ain't seen him in over fifty years now.' (*Imitates* REDHEAD:) 'Oh it's fine, Elvis – goin' a bit grey, mind, lookin' forward to gettin' a pension, but –'

REDHEAD: I couldn't tell him then – it was right after his daddy had that big heart attack.

MARTY: Well, can't someone tell him now – just say he kicked it – kinda peaceful like – just slipped off to that Great Tree in the Sky – his last words were, 'Goodbye Boss, I'm off to see Old Shep.'
(*They start giggling.* MARIE-ANNE *listens disbelieving.*)

JO JO: Only reason he's never found out is cos he's so terrified of hospitals he won't go an' visit the mutt . . .

(JO JO *looks up and sees that the* DOCTOR *has just arrived silently in the room, looking like a Boston lawyer with an excess of jewellery and an attaché case. He stands watching them – but not for long.*)

DOCTOR: He'll just want more and more real medication, you know, if you keep giving him placebos –

MARTY: Get out of here – get the hell out of here! Go on, get out – or I'll give you a placebo with a blowtorch.

DOCTOR: (*Evenly*) *You* called me.

MARTY: The date's off – I don't love you any more.

JO JO: An' anyway, he's a married man.

MARTY: NOW GET OUT!

(MARTY *picks up the machine-gun.* MARIE-ANNE *moves behind him, puts the tray on the table.*)

Is this thing loaded?

JO JO: Could find out.

DOCTOR: (*Calmly*) I'll leave the prescription with (*points off*) Charlie.

MARTY: Yeah, you do that – and one of these days I'll leave your brains on the ceiling.

JO JO: (*Evenly*) Because you know you – you're takin' him so far down, when he finally goes, he won't need buryin'.

DOCTOR: I'm keepin' him alive.

MARTY: Y' CALL THIS LIVIN'?

(*He scatters some of the pills and excess with the barrel of the machine-gun.* REDHEAD *moves forward and tries for the formality of a genteel Southern lady.*)

REDHEAD: Excuse me, I would like you to go now, Doctor Rocco, and any prescriptions you leave my fiancé will be dealt with after you have gone.

JO JO: Yeah, we'll rip the bastards up.

(*The* DOCTOR *turns away, moves away, turns back.*)

DOCTOR: He'll go somewhere else, boys, Elvis always does. And some of the so-called doctors I know, that should really worry you.

(*He smiles warmly at them, turns as if to go.* MARTY *moves past* REDHEAD, *snarls an obscenity and presses the trigger of the machine-gun – instinctively. Bullets fly with whatever sound*

36

and visual effects that can be achieved. The spurt of bullets narrowly misses the DOCTOR, *who throws himself to the ground.* MARIE-ANNE *and* REDHEAD *scream and throw themselves to the ground – to be joined by* JO JO. MARTY *drops the machine-gun in absolute horror and leans against the table in shock.*)

MARTY: Ah. Ahhhhh. Hmmmmm.

(*The* DOCTOR, *grabbing his attaché case, goes out of the room on his hands and knees.*)

Look what I done. Oh . . . Shhhit!

(REDHEAD *and* JO JO *climb to their feet, go to* MARTY *and hold him as he begins to slide down on to the floor. They put him in a chair. He looks at the damage.* MARIE-ANNE *has taken the tray and moves across the room, examines the 'damage' closely.*)

MARIE-ANNE: I knew I should have stayed working in that old people's home . . .

(*She goes off.*)

MARTY: Give me a pill. Quick. Better give me two . . .

(*He means it till he sees the irony. Laughs. Still wants a pill.*)

Look at those goddamn bullet holes . . .

JO JO: Don't worry, they'll just merge in with all the others . . .

MARTY: (*Holding a pill box*) He always slows down after these, doesn't he?

JO JO: He used to.

MARTY: Do me, man. (*Takes two, adds another, drinks.*) Christ, Jo Jo, I parted his hair, swear to God, gotta centre part now . . .

JO JO: Yeah . . . Y' know y've just took three aspirin there?

(*They both start laughing.* JO JO *stops, picks up the gun.*)

Y' know what he'll be doin' now – forcin' Charlie to take the stuff – 'Get this stuff to him and don't tell the other two.'

(*Both* MEN *stand and move towards the doors,* JO JO *with gun.*)

REDHEAD: I'm going to tell him, I am, I'm going to tell him to his face, he's not to have any more of those placebos . . .

(*Giggles from the two* MEN *as they go.*)

37

What's the matter, boys . . . ?

DUKE *and* GERRY *and the* ENGLISHMAN.
DUKE *has moved to the chair by the phone. He is talking into the telephone, quietly, easily. The* OTHER TWO *watch from the table (with added beer bottles). The* ENGLISHMAN *has the lid off the battery part of the tape recorder.*

DUKE: . . . nothin' serious, Charlie, just old times – got our signals crossed a little there before . . . The book? (*Glances across.*) Well sure yeah, if he wants to talk about the book, we'd just like to talk about . . . it's only the truth, Charlie, that's all, just a little book, an' it need never be written, if you get my drift. All we need is a few words with the man . . . (*Looks again towards the others. Smiles.*) All night, we'll be here all night . . . *I don't want any lectures, all right – he started this.* (*Puts the phone down abruptly. Leans back.*) You got any whisky?

ENGLISHMAN: (*Nods.*) In the car. I'll get it in a minute. He will call, won't he?

DUKE: Oh he'll call all right. The message has been received.

ENGLISHMAN: You do know what to say?

DUKE: Sure – the question is – will he know what to say? (*Walks across.*) Ain't you fixed that yet? (*He examines the empty beer bottles.*)

ENGLISHMAN: It's er working now. The batteries must have . . .

DUKE: You been to one of them English universities?

GERRY: Oxford?

ENGLISHMAN: Well . . . a university, yes, but not Oxford.

GERRY: You an intellectual?

ENGLISHMAN: No no!

DUKE: You can't work a tape recorder – you must be.

ENGLISHMAN: I'm just a writer –

DUKE: What does an intellectual want with a Southern boy?

ENGLISHMAN: I'm not an intellectual – but is it important?

GERRY: Is indeed, son. Intellectuals carry a sneer around with them. It's not there on their faces but up there in their . . . brains.

38

DUKE: About people like us.

GERRY: White trash.

DUKE: You a Jew?

ENGLISHMAN: Would it matter?

DUKE: Not to us it wouldn't, but I bet it would to you.

ENGLISHMAN: I still don't see –

DUKE: Don't assume – all right – don't. Cos listen, I take a
    shower every day, I shake my pecker with every piss, I
    don't chew tabaccy an' niggahs are fine by me, even when
    they're not in their place.

GERRY: An' he hardly ever beats his woman. Not even when he
    has a perfect right to.

DUKE: *All right?*

ENGLISHMAN: Certainly. Gentlemen.

DUKE: Still haven't answered the question. *What do you want
    with him?* Why're you here?

ENGLISHMAN: Because –

DUKE: Apart from the money.

ENGLISHMAN: Because he is the nearest thing to a Greek god
    that our generation – (*shrugs*) – this century will ever see.

GERRY: He ain't never been to Greece.

Gracelands. The Viewing Room.
The OLDER PRESLEY *re-enters.* REDHEAD *is alone.*

OLDER PRESLEY: Duke and Gerry wanna talk to me. (*Laughs
    harshly.*)

REDHEAD: I want to talk to you, and then I'm retiring.

OLDER PRESLEY: Wanna gold watch? Cadillac? Wha' d'y' want,
    honey?

REDHEAD: Nothing. I just want to talk to you.

OLDER PRESLEY: Yeah, sure, see you later, hon. Got things to
    do.
    (*He again reaches out for and opens the attaché case.*
    REDHEAD *slams the case lid down.*)

REDHEAD: And that's what I want to talk about – it's too much
    – too much – I can't take any more –

OLDER PRESLEY: (*Coldly*) You don't take them.

REDHEAD: Well, if you think I'm . . . I'm . . . well, I'm not,

39

I'm not – you got so much, Elvis, you've got everything anyone could ever wish for – and live for – and you've got your daughter and all – you want to be there when she grows up – well, well . . . well, you're not going to be if you keep on.

(*She moves away from him. He grabs hold of her arm.*)

OLDER PRESLEY: I got a daughter. Yeah . . . now tell me what else I got.

REDHEAD: Oh! Self-pity ain't no pity at all – it's just pitiful.

OLDER PRESLEY: You wanna leave me, yeah, you leave me, you leave me like Lisa Marie'll leave me, like all the others left me, like my mama left me, like Jesse left me, like Priscilla left me, like those bastards Duke and Gerry left me, but they're gonna come crawlin' back under those gates, like you'll come crawlin' back too.

(*She moves away from him.*)

Get your bags packed. Get out of my house. Get lost. Get ill. Get . . . get . . . (*Grabs the attaché case and hurls it open, grabs a handful of pills. Sits huddled, holding the pills. Then finally throws them away.*) Oh mama. Mama.

We see the YOUNGER PRESLEY, *lying on his bed above, looking out of a window, red jacket thrown on the bed, and we hear the voice of his* MOTHER.

GLADYS PRESLEY: Elvis . . . Elvis! What you doin' up there, son?

(*She enters the room, sees him, laughs.*)

You still starin' at that car?

YOUNGER PRESLEY: Cadillac, mama. That's no ordinary car. That's a Cadillac. It's bright pink, it's nearly new, and it's all mine!

GLADYS PRESLEY: You just gonna look at it – or are you gonna drive it at all?

YOUNGER PRESLEY: (*Laughing*) I'll get to that – right now I'm just lookin'. (*Looks further out of the window.*) There ain't a Cadillac on the block, mama.

GLADYS PRESLEY: I'm not surprised – there's barely a car on the block . . . We don't live in Cadillac country.

(PRESLEY *finally turns around. He gets off the bed.* GLADYS *sits on it.*)

YOUNGER PRESLEY: But we will, mama, we will. You an' daddy an' me, we're goin' to have the finest house in all of Memphis. We're going to have a mansion in Memphis! (*She laughs.*)

You'll be laughin' all right, when I'm carryin' you in my arms down that driveway – two new Cadillacs parked outside – maid an' butler at the door –

(BOTH *now laughing together.*)

Ahh mama, believe me – look – (*kneels on the bed*) – one little record that only made the Country charts – an' look what it got me – (*points outside*) – Memphis bought me that – America's gonna buy me the world!

(*They both laugh uproariously. He whoops for joy.*)

GLADYS PRESLEY: Chandeliers.

YOUNGER PRESLEY: What d'y' mean?

GLADYS PRESLEY: Can I have chandeliers? In that house. Always wanted chandeliers.

YOUNGER PRESLEY: Every room – even the broom cupboard and the john – garage too. Open the fridge – little light'll be a chandelier!

(*They fall about laughing. She moves away from* PRESLEY, *turns back, speaks quietly, plainly.*)

GLADYS PRESLEY: And when that day comes, son, we'll go down to the Pentecostal Church and give thanks to God, and then we'll walk down to the riverside where Jesse was laid to rest, carried by your daddy, buried by the Welfare in the cheapest baby box that they could find, no cross nor marker nor gold letters on marble; never would have found it again if I hadn't have left my handkerchief there . . . beneath a stone . . . and . . . and Jesse will look down, son, and he'll be proud – he'll be there – he'll be with you – he ain't never left me – he ain't never left you.

YOUNGER PRESLEY: I know that, mama.

(*He reaches out for her, holds her – mother and son.*)

And when we go down to that river that fine day, you're goin' to find the biggest monument made of marble and

41

gold letters that you ever did see!
(*He kisses her forehead and lets her go. As the lights go down, he returns to his view of his Cadillac.*)

The OLDER PRESLEY – *alone, again.*

OLDER PRESLEY: And I did, I got lucky and we had them chandeliers, and I took my mama down to the riverside like I said I would, Jesse. (*Half laughs.*) An' the Cadillac blew up a week later, doin' a hundred and five – Cape Canaveral sent out an alert!
(*He sees* REDHEAD *at the doorway.*)
You won't ever leave me, will y' . . . ?
(*She shakes her head, moves towards him.*)
I'm in a lot of pain . . . you know that, don't you?

REDHEAD: Of course I do.

OLDER PRESLEY: I need this stuff to take the pain away. That's all. And then sometimes, just occasionally (*Smiles mockingly*), I need it so I can forget . . . Forget.
(PRESLEY *looks at* REDHEAD, *demanding a reply.*)

REDHEAD: Forget what?

OLDER PRESLEY: I can't remember. (*Grins at her.*) It was great. Great. All of it. (*Laughs.*) I ain't never laughed so much in all my life . . . before or since . . . than I did then. In 'fifty-six. Before it all . . . I miss my mama, Reds. Can't stop thinkin' –

REDHEAD: Ssshhh. Ssshhh.

OLDER PRESLEY: My mama died.

REDHEAD: Ssshhh, ssshhh, all right baby.

OLDER PRESLEY: A day ago. *Yesterday.*

REDHEAD: (*Alarmed*) No no –

OLDER PRESLEY: A day ago. Nineteen years ago yesterday. August the fourteenth, 'fifty-eight. I wasn't there, honey. I was . . . somewhere else. I was where I didn't wanna be. I was in the US Army.

REDHEAD: You weren't to – you couldn't –

OLDER PRESLEY: And I wasn't. Missed it. You only get one chance. No rehearsals. You're either there on the night – or you're not. And I wasn't.

(*She goes to hold him tighter.*)
No it's all right – just tellin' you.
REDHEAD: (*Touches his lips with her fingers.*) The Colonel keeps phoning – that's why I –
OLDER PRESLEY: What?
REDHEAD: *The Colonel.* On your phone by the bedside.
OLDER PRESLEY: So? War's been declared? Again.
REDHEAD: It's every two minutes, honey, I can't get to sleep, and he sounds as mad as hell.
OLDER PRESLEY: Take the phone off the hook . . . or tell him to go to hell.
(*She stays with him.*)

COLONEL PARKER *with a set of accounts and books all over his desk.*
He slams the phone down and phones again.
COLONEL: Vernon, get in here, I wanna . . . I don't care what time it is, y' can walk ten yards any time of the day an' night – just get in here – wanna talk to you about that son of yours.
(*He throws the phone down. Phones again, briefly. Throws that phone down, as he uses a calculator savagely.* VERNON *hurries in, slightly misdressed, carrying a file.*)
You read those figures?
(VERNON *barely has time to nod.*)
The boy's got to be told.
VERNON PRESLEY: I already told him.
COLONEL: He's got to be told again. (*Pointedly*) And not just for his own sake . . .
VERNON PRESLEY: (*Points at the accounts. Nervously*) You sure you haven't missed somethin' out somewhere, Colonel? You know, the odd coupla million . . . (*Laughs – inevitably alone.*)
COLONEL: OK. (*Pulls the books towards him.*) Let's start again – an' don't count on your fingers, Vernon, it kinda embarrasses me . . .
(VERNON PRESLEY *scowls into the books.*)

DUKE *and* GERRY, *bored and thirsty, and the* ENGLISHMAN.

DUKE: You seen him recently?

ENGLISHMAN: I've been trying. It's hard to get through the Colonel.

DUKE: A bullet might work.
(*Mirthless laughter.*)

ENGLISHMAN: I've made some contacts but – and now with you two . . .

DUKE: You see him *on stage*?

ENGLISHMAN: Yes, I've seen him.

DUKE: Recent?

ENGLISHMAN: Las Vegas, some months ago. (*Looks away.*)

GERRY: And?

ENGLISHMAN: He . . . held the audience. Spellbound. Thousands . . . and thousands watched and adored . . . and never saw at all.

DUKE: Meanin' what?

ENGLISHMAN: It means he's a god. To many people.

DUKE: Very good. Now why don't you go and get the whisky?
(*The* ENGLISHMAN *moves away from them.*)
Asshole.

GERRY: Yeah . . . how do you think god's gonna take all this?

DUKE: We'll find out soon enough.

The viewing room at Gracelands.

The OLDER PRESLEY *with* REDHEAD *close to him.*

OLDER PRESLEY: Yeah well . . . I'm going to have to . . . if I'm *ever* gonna win . . . or even understand . . . dream of a better land . . . just face myself once in a while . . . I've gotta face the facts, tell the truth, if only to myself . . .
(*He looks towards* REDHEAD, *who has listened with sympathy if no real understanding, but with a willingness, as ever, to help.*)
You must be tired . . . I'm sorry, honey, if I've . . . why don't you get off, get your head down?

REDHEAD: I don't mind stayin', honey, if –

OLDER PRESLEY: I'll be all right . . . might even . . . coupla songs been on my mind, might even play myself a little late

44

night music. (*That smile again.*) See you later. Alligator.
(*She stands and leaves, exhausted and relieved . . . yet . . .*
PRESLEY *slides the guitar off the table towards himself, then
reaches for the telephone, stops.*)
Later, later, when I'm ready. They're gonna crawl. *Crawl.*
Back to the King. (*Turns to the other throne at his side.
Smiles.*) I wanna ask you one question, Jesse. I wanna ask
you this – who is the most famous person in the world –
right – it's either me or Mohammed Ali – well, maybe it
might be him – he's a nice guy an' I like him – *but* he
cheated – no man, he did – the bastard's got the Third
World in his pocket – all that Muslim mumbo-jumbo –
religion comes free but y' need money in y' pocket to buy
my records, and the Third World ain't got no money – so I
don't care if they never heard of me – so all right, take
away the starvin' – an' I know that sounds cruel, Jesse –
but take them away anyway – an' what're y' left with – y'
left with me. I am the most famous person in the world.
I'm not braggin', brother – that's a fact – an' . . . *But what
did I do wrong?* That's what I wanna know. (*Hits the table.*)
Paid my taxes, paid my dues, bit my lip, one polite boy, yes
sir, no sir, when they said jump, I said, 'How high, sir!'
Didn't have to. Could've been sorted. (*Clicks his fingers.*)
'Take Care of Business' . . . Could've died in there, Jesse.
Yes, sir. Come out after two years a rock 'n' roll *corpse*.
Didn't have to suffer that, *I was Elvis Presley.*
(*The lights dim on Gracelands.*)

*A crowded press conference – as crowded as it can be . . .
The* YOUNGER PRESLEY *fielding questions with an innocent
warmth. And charm. As the scene starts, we are aware of three
shadows at the rear. Identifiable finally as a high-ranking* US ARMY
OFFICER, COLONEL PARKER *and then the* OLDER PRESLEY.
FIRST REPORTER: Would you say, Elvis, that your method of
    singing and dancing is deliberately intended to incite an
    audience to a state of cataclysmic ecstasy?
YOUNGER PRESLEY: Pardon. Sir?
    (*The* OLDER PRESLEY *moves forward slightly, animated and*

loving, laughing – for the time being.)

OLDER PRESLEY: Pardon sir! Pardon sir – Christ man, talk about polite! They could have sat on your face an' all you would have done is hold your breath.

SECOND REPORTER: They're burnin' your records in the Bible Belt – what do you think about that?

YOUNGER PRESLEY: Yeah, my manager told me my records were hot in Alabama – thought it was good news at first! (*Laughter.*)

THIRD REPORTER: What do you say though, Elvis, to the likes of Billy Graham – calling you a danger to the fabric of society – a degenerate influence on the younger generation?

YOUNGER PRESLEY: I'd say a lot if I knew what he meant. (*More laughter.*)
Ladies an' gentlemen, I just go out there an' sing my songs. Don't like 'em – don't buy 'em.

ASSHOLE REPORTER: What about the Army?

YOUNGER PRESLEY: (*Quickly*) Oh I just love someone in uniform, don't you?

OLDER PRESLEY: (*Laughing*) Christ, I don't remember that!

ASSHOLE REPORTER: You tryin' to dodge the draft, or somethin'?

YOUNGER PRESLEY: I ain't never dodged nothin' – 'cept a couple of mean line-backers in high school.

ASSHOLE REPORTER: You don't want to go in the Army though, do you?
(*For the first time we hear the slight stammer that Presley had in public when he was nervous.*)

YOUNGER PRESLEY: What I want's got nothin' t' . . . t'do with it. I'm an American male citizen – I'll take what's comin'.

ASSHOLE REPORTER: But rumour has it, Elvis, you're tryin' for draft exclusion.

YOUNGER PRESLEY: Rumour is wrong. (*Looks towards* COLONEL PARKER.) Next question. I thought we were here to talk about my singin' – I'll sing an army song for you if you want. *Next question*.

ASSHOLE REPORTER: Say you got called up tomorrow, Elvis,

what would you do?

(*The* YOUNGER PRESLEY *turns towards* COLONEL PARKER *for help.* PARKER *approaches, while the* ARMY OFFICER *stays in the background.* COLONEL PARKER *stands alongside the* YOUNGER PRESLEY, *avuncular and protecting, as the posse of* JOURNALISTS *surrounds the* YOUNGER PRESLEY, *so that we cannot see him. As* PARKER *does this, the* OLDER PRESLEY *steps forward, at a different angle. The questions and answers go into mute form as the* OLDER PRESLEY *talks.*)

OLDER PRESLEY: See, they all had daughters, Jesse, and sons who suddenly had sideburns and quiffs – an' they thought I was dangerous. (*Laughs.*) Gonna turn their dreams into nightmares – gonna question their authority – all the authorities – some kind of rebel – a rebel! I ain't never rebelled in my whole goddamn life.

ASSHOLE REPORTER: But come on, what you rebellin' against, son?

OLDER PRESLEY: (*Brando in* The Wild Ones:) 'What you got?' (*Turns away.*) Not me, no not me, I might have been different – man, I was different – but I wasn't a rebel – all I knew about rebels, Jesse, was locked up in the Civil War. (*He walks through the scene towards* PARKER, *reaches the crowd around* YOUNGER PRESLEY, *reaches down and appears to run his hand affectionately through the* YOUNGER PRESLEY's *hair as he goes past. Barely all we can see is the hair as he is crowded and surrounded by the journalists.*)

(*As the scene develops*) Yeah, the Colonel – don't look like nothin', does he? Hah – wanna know what I see? I see a man who painted sparrows yellow and sold them as canaries – see a man who never really loved anyone – biggest turn-on he ever had was probably a hundred-dollar bill with a hole in the middle – (*laughs*) – see a man who's so fat, his toilet's so big, there's wild ducks on the water. (*Laughs. Stops.*) But he was waitin' for me – an' maybe I was waitin' for him . . .

(*The* ARMY OFFICER *approaches the crowd around the* YOUNGER PRESLEY *holding a US army private's uniform like a religious robe. The* CROWD *parts with reverence.* PARKER *is*

closely holding a dummy of the YOUNGER PRESLEY, *sitting
him on one knee.* PARKER *controls the dummy so that it looks
up towards him, swivelling its head like Archie Andrews.*
PARKER *nods his head, shakes the dummy.* 'Younger Presley'
nods. The ARMY OFFICER *lays the uniform across the dummy
of Younger Presley.*)

COLONEL: You wanna meet Frank Sinatra and the President,
don't you, son?
(*The dummy is forced to nod vigorously.*)

Gracelands. The viewing room.
The OLDER PRESLEY *approaching both thrones, spins 'Jesse's'
around.*

OLDER PRESLEY: But the last thing I wanted to do was go in
that man's army – two years in some lousy Kraut stinkhole,
bein' one of the boys – *I ain't never been one of the boys!*
(*Grabs a handful of pills and swallows them, drinking milk.*)
Ahhh, you're better off out of it, Jesse . . . (*Sits down, the
guitar in hand.*) Come on, Jesse, why didn't you live? What
were you doin' in there . . . Oh, if you'd have lived, man, if
you'd have lived, we could've been the Everly Brothers.
(*Laughs. Stops, suddenly low and down.*) You could've been
King . . . you could've won, could've had the rainbows and
the dreams and the gold, and it wouldn't have hurt you.
Cos I always thought . . . I really believed . . . that this . . .
THIS – (*waves his arms around*) this would have made me
happy. Ever after. That it would have made it all all right
. . . Mama. (*Stands up, the guitar near to hand.*) Mama.
Come on, mama, come back and stand up for me, tell
them, mama, I was a good boy, I was the best, I was good,
an' they're gonna tell the world that I wasn't, an' that I'm
not, but *I am*! good . . . Just took too much. Since you've
been gone. Standin' here, mama, standin' up straight,
tryin' to face myself. Need to face you as well. Face the
day I broke down an' cried an' tried to climb in there with
you . . . come on, come on, couldn't face you . . . goin'
away then – gotta face it now, cos I've gotta *live* . . .
There's got to be – (*laughs*) – gotta be some way of gettin'

out of this ahead . . . I am Elvis Presley.
(*We see him turn to face briefly the funeral images parading at
the back of the stage. We see the cortège and the totally bereft
slumping supported* YOUNGER PRESLEY. *We hear 'Peace in
the Valley'*)

Oh well, I'm so tired and so weary
But I must go along.
Till the Land Comes and calls,
Calls be away, oh yes.

(*And the* OLDER PRESLEY *begins to sing 'If I Can Dream',
getting stronger and more affirmative as the song proceeds.
And the black shadows at the back become a colourful
passionate life-force chorus. A victory against the night.
Perhaps only the* YOUNGER PRESLEY *stays in black and
kneels, almost curled up in his grief.*)

There must be lights burning brighter somewhere,
Got to be birds flying higher in a sky more blue,
If I can dream of a better land,
With my brother walking hand in hand,
Tell me why, oh why oh why can't my dreams come
    true?
Oh why?

There must be peace and understanding sometime,
Strong winds of promise that will blow away the doubt
    and fear,
If I can dream of a warmer sun,
Where hope keeps shining on everyone,
Tell me why, oh why, oh why won't that sun appear?

I'm lost in a cloud with too much rain,
I'm trapped in a world that's troubled with pain,
(*Looks back.*)
But as long as a man has the strength to dream,
He can redeem his soul and fly.

Deep in my heart there's a trembling question,
Still I am sure that the answer's, the answer's gonna
    come somehow,

Out there in the dark there's a beckoning candle,
And while I can feel, while I can talk,
While I can stand, while I can walk,
While I can dream,
I feel that my dream can come true
Right now!
(*Lights out.*)

ACT TWO

The viewing room at Gracelands.
The OLDER PRESLEY *at the piano as the curtain lifts and the lights come on. Relaxed, playing a gentle version of 'All My Trials, Lord'.*
REDHEAD, MARTY *and* JO JO *listening and enjoying every peaceful moment.*

OLDER PRESLEY:
>   If living were a thing that money could buy,
>   You know the rich would live and the poor would die,
>   All my trials, Lord, soon be over . . .
>   . . . So hush little baby, don't you cry,
>   You know your daddy's bound to die,
>   But all my trials, Lord, soon be over . . .
>   . . . Oh I wish I was in Dixie,
>   In the land of cotton,
>   Old times there are not forgotten,
>   Look away, look away, look away, Dixieland . . .
>   (*Happy days are here again, as he moves from the piano.*)

OLDER PRESLEY: Just give me the singing. I'm all right when I'm singing. (*Turns to* REDHEAD.) I feel . . . I feel . . . 'I feel pretty and witty and gay . . .' (*Breaks up, laughing. Turns to the* BOYS.) Remember that faggot in 'fifty-six? (*Brief blank from the* OTHER TWO.)
The television producer – before they tried to ban me from the neck down.

JO JO: Oh yeah – yeah!
(*The* THREE MEN *start laughing.*)

OLDER PRESLEY: I never told you about this guy, Reds. (*Laughs, shakes his head.*) It was about the time when all those little girls were goin' mad about me. When I first started. Didn't know what I was doin' – certainly didn't know what I was doin' to them – just movin' to the music – just did it an' laughed – I was gettin' paid for doin' *this* –

51

an' I laughed so hard the tears ran right down their legs –
an' then when I knew what it was I was doin' – I did it even
more – an' I never laughed so much in all my life. Never
thought it was going to stop. But that television show – I'm
telling you! Let's see that again, hey?

JO JO: (*Into the intercom*) Run the faggot.

OLDER PRESLEY: Nobody ever did what I was doin' then.
(*Laughs.*) But I didn't show them nothing' in rehearsal –
walked through it, when I wasn't standin' still an' bein'
polite – that pretty-boy producer wonderin' what all the
fuss was about – wasn't turned on by me at all – expectin'
some kind of rock 'n' roll James Dean – got Pat Boone
instead. In rehearsal. And then . . . (*Grins at* REDHEAD.
Puts his arm around her.) And then . . .

A television show.
The ANNOUNCER *at the side. A 1950s television camera and*
CAMERAMAN. *The* TELEVISION PRODUCER *stares out of a*
window in a control booth and occasionally looks down at what we
presume to be his console. He is not, by any means, a totally limp-
wristed man – more 'New York Gay'.

ANNOUNCER: And now, ladies and gentlemen, boys and . . .
especially you girls, the moment you've all been waiting for
– the one and only new singing sensation – Elvis Presley!
(*The camera moves away towards where the* YOUNGER
PRESLEY *stands – at his most erotic, vital and graphic yet*
loving every second and hardly able to contain his laughter.
Nothing obscene – just good old healthy standing up simulated
sex with an audience of millions of strangers. He sings 'Hound
Dog'.)

YOUNGER PRESLEY:
You ain't nothin' but a hound dog,
Crockin' all the time,
You ain't nothin' but a hound dog,
Crockin' all the time,
Well, you ain't never caught a rabbit,
And you ain't no friend of mine.

Well, they said you was high class,
Well, that was just a lie,
Yeah, they said you was high class,
Well, that was just a lie,
Yeah, you ain't never caught a rabbit,
And you ain't no friend of mine.
You ain't nothin' but a hound dog,
Crockin' all the time,
You ain't never caught a rabbit,
And you ain't no friend of mine.

Well, they said you were high class,
But that was just a lie,
You know they said you were high class,
But that was just a lie,
Well, you ain't never caught a rabbit
And you ain't no friend of mine.
You ain't nothin' but a hound dog,
Crockin' all the time,
Well, you ain't never caught a rabbit,
You ain't no friend of mine.

(*Simultaneously: the developing levels of hysteria reached by the* PRODUCER *as* PRESLEY *reaches for an outrageous climax to the song, partly in the instrumental break.*)

PRODUCER: Oh my God! What's he doin'? Fucking Jerusalem! He's – he's . . . doing . . . *it*! He's out there fucking. He's . . . that's fucking! He's fucking in front of the fucking camera – he's fucking in 50 million living rooms – (*Screams instructions through the intercom to the* CAMERAMAN:) Get away from his fucking body – close in, close in f'Christ's sake – just give me his head – (*Looks around.*) What is funny? What is fucking funny? Just get in close on his face . . . Jesus, even his face is fucking . . .

(*The* PRODUCER *stares out of the control booth as* PRESLEY *finishes singing and runs off – into history. The phone rings in the control booth.*)

And now for a word from our sponsors . . . No, four words: 'You'll never work again . . .' (*Picks up the phone as*

the lights go down on him.) Hello . . . it's funny you should
say that, sir . . .

The viewing room. Gracelands.

OLDER PRESLEY: (*Extremely happy*) Yeah, banned from the
neck down. Had to wiggle my ears. (*Again fingers the piece
of paper*.) Well. The time has come to talk of many things.
As someone once said to someone else. In some poem I
read. Sometime.

JO JO: It's gone midnight you know, boss.

OLDER PRESLEY: So – who's askin' you? An' anyway, neither
of them's Cinderella.

REDHEAD: Just –

OLDER PRESLEY: But I sure as hell been their fairy godmother.
(*He begins to dial the number, makes a mess of it first time, then
tries again. He has to put his face close to the paper and the
phone to see*.)

Simultaneously: DUKE *and* GERRY *and the* ENGLISHMAN – *very
overtired*.

ENGLISHMAN: Those early days –

DUKE: Great days.

GERRY: No shit out of Elvis then – none inside him neither –
wouldn't even take a headache tablet – two bottles of beer,
had to carry him home.

ENGLISHMAN: So Presley hasn't always been – he didn't have
to . . . or even want to indulge his sexual fantasies the way
he does now – not when he was a . . . young man.

DUKE: Can y' keep it simple – it's gettin' late.
(*The* ENGLISHMAN *looks at his watch, then speaks into the
tape*.)

ENGLISHMAN: August the sixteenth, 1977.

GERRY: What's that for?

ENGLISHMAN: So I'll know where I am.

DUKE: We coulda told you where you are – you're here with us.

ENGLISHMAN: No, you know, later when I'm cross-refer–
(*The phone rings. They stop being overtired.* DUKE *races to the
phone.* GERRY *races to the other one.* DUKE *picks it up, putting
the recorder on as well*.)

54

DUKE: Yeah?

Gracelands. The viewing room.
The OLDER PRESLEY *holds, smiling. Finally speaks with great warmth.*
OLDER PRESLEY: Duke, it's Elvis. (*Laughs.*) Listen, man, you do anything you want – I don't care – but there's just one thing you could do for me.
DUKE: Yeah?
OLDER PRESLEY: Yeah. Go screw yourself. Sideways.
 (PRESLEY *puts the phone down – one happy laughing man.*)
REDHEAD: Oh baby . . .
OLDER PRESLEY: Good for him – he's comin' back, better get used to what he's gonna get.
JO JO: Well, he'd better come back . . .
OLDER PRESLEY: *Meaning what?*
JO JO: (*Uneasily*) Just . . . he'd better come back. (*Shrugs.*)
OLDER PRESLEY: Always take your place, man.
 (*The atmosphere goes sour and down.* JO JO *looks towards* MARTY *and shakes his head.*)

DUKE *and* GERRY *and the* ENGLISHMAN.
DUKE: *Bastard.*
ENGLISHMAN: It's a start.
GERRY: Yeah. Sounded friendly enough.
 (DUKE *looks at him in disbelief and disgust, approaches the table.*)
DUKE: *Bastard.* I'll make him . . . I'll spill so many fuckin' beans, the fuckin' book'll fart. 'Bout time we stopped bein' generous with that asshole. You want filth, that what you want? You want the real bad goods? You got sickness and pus, pornography and drugs and all that stuff – that ain't nothin' – just pimples and boils compared with this. (*Takes a piece of paper out of a pocket, hurls it on the table.*) That's a tumour you've got there on the table. And it's malignant.
 (*The* ENGLISHMAN *carefully unfolds it, begins to read, quickly looks up at* DUKE, *looks down again.* DUKE *paces madly about.*)

55

Huh. *Huh!* I got you, I got you, man, you boy, you are
pinned down, send for the microscope – let everyone see –
cos I got you, let's see you, son, got you, oh yes, *got you*.
(*The* ENGLISHMAN *glances up at* DUKE *as he manics on*.)

ENGLISHMAN: He wrote this?

DUKE: All on his own. Even joined all the letters up. Full stops
an' all.

ENGLISHMAN: It's a photostat.

DUKE: You expect the real thing, f'Christ's sake? That's my
pension, boy, an' it's been sittin' in the bank just waitin' to
be collected.

ENGLISHMAN: But why did you save this till now?

DUKE: Never you mind.

ENGLISHMAN: You were still hoping to go back, weren't you?
Back to Gracelands, all is forgiven. Welcome back. On the
payroll again.

DUKE: I'd shut up if I were you, mack.

ENGLISHMAN: I was just part of the game plan -- bit of dirt and
bile and gossip. I was only the bait.

DUKE: Yeah, a worm. (*Thrusts the paper directly in front of the*
ENGLISHMAN *and presses the tape recorder buttons*.) There's
no goin' back now. Not for any of us.

ENGLISHMAN: (*Reads:*) 'I promise never to do anything terrible
like this again, I promise never to harbour violent thoughts
like these again, I promise never to hurt, in any way shape
or form, my Priscilla, I promise to look after my little Lisa
Marie all my life, I promise never to try and get Mike Stone
killed ever ever again, I promise, I promise, I hereby
promise. I swear to God on everything I hold sacred.'
(*The* ENGLISHMAN *pushes the paper away from himself,*
switches the tape recorder off.)
You know, all the things you've told me about him, for
good or for bad, nothing at all touched me – till that.
(*Indicates the paper*.) There's nothing but pain and sorrow in
every word.

DUKE: Yeah well, save all that for the funeral.
(*The* ENGLISHMAN *looks with total contempt at* DUKE, *who*
stares back. GERRY *taps the* ENGLISHMAN *gently on the arm*.)

56

GERRY: (*Mildly*) If you want out, you can get out. (*Smiles.*)
Plenty of other writers. Really. Betcha ass they'd jump at
this . . .
ENGLISHMAN: (*After an age*) Do you want to tell me what
exactly happened?
(*The lights fade down on them as* DUKE *sits down – victorious.*)

Gracelands. The viewing room.
The OLDER PRESLEY *being consoled and cheered by* REDHEAD.
MARTY *and* JO JO *dozing on to their arms.*
OLDER PRESLEY: Maybe I should call Duke back, you know,
tell him it was a joke . . . Christ, don't all answer at
once . . .
REDHEAD: Tell me again about 'fifty-six, honey.
OLDER PRESLEY: (*Sighs.*) Before you were born, Reds . . .
REDHEAD: My mama remembers though –
OLDER PRESLEY: Send her along. (*Half laughs, perks up
slightly.*) She didn't get to meet me ever, did she?
REDHEAD: I've told you, sweetheart, one night in Idaho she
nearly got to touch you as you –
OLDER PRESLEY: 'S all right. Just a wild thought. (*Grins
towards* MARTY *and* JO JO, *who are out of it.*) There's
nothin' else to tell you 'bout 'fifty-six, nothin' else I'd care
to tell you anyway, same with 'fifty-seven, just out there
havin' a ball, one long party . . . and then the party was
over. Ten wasted years, baby. 'Fifty-eight to 'sixty-eight.
Two years in the Army, and eight years in Hollywood. Hah
. . . went in wantin' to be Marlon Brando, came out like
the Tin Man in *Over the Rainbow*. Made five thousand and
five films with a curled lip and a blank mind. 'Yes Colonel,
no, Colonel, thank you, Colonel, that was the pits, Colonel,
the scripts are gettin' worse, Colonel . . . oh I see, the
money's gettin' better, oh well, that's all right, what's the
next one – ah I get to fall in love with a nun – great.'
(*Laughs in a tired manner.*) And the songs – Jesus, the
songs – how can a grown man sing a song about clam fishin'
as if it was 'Love Me Tender'? This grown man did.
(*Sings:*) 'Love me tender, love me clam – don't clam up,

57

don't you know who I am?'

(*She giggles. He laughs, tired yet happy now – too happy.*)

Yeah well, I took it, didn't I, Reds, sat here and broke my heart . . . saw me an' mama, you know, an' came through. 'Fifty-eight. Can go anywhere now, if I can dream. (*Looks at her.*) Ever tell you about Cilla. And me?

(JO JO *and* MARTY *are jolted from their near slumbers, exchange glances sideways, slowly begin 'casually' to sit up.*)

REDHEAD: You always said, honey, that I wasn't to –

OLDER PRESLEY: Loved that little girl. In my fashion. Don't mind do you, babe?

REDHEAD: (*Genuinely*) No, no. What's done is done.

OLDER PRESLEY: And that's done. For. Boy, is that done for. (*He suddenly hits the table with his fist. Everyone jumps into action.*)

MARTY: 'Sixty-eight!

JO JO: Yeah! (*Whispers:*) What?

REDHEAD: Sweetheart, I don't really –

MARTY: Said you could go anywhere, boss – go to 'sixty-eight. Do not stop. That Christmas special! (*Whistles.*) What a show!

JO JO: The King is Back!

OLDER PRESLEY: Yeah.

MARTY: I'll get it put on. (*Reaches for and mutters into the intercom.*)

OLDER PRESLEY: Colonel wanted me to sing Christmas songs. Know that? 'Rudolph the Red-nosed Reindeer.' An hour of that – imagine? Clams an' fuckin' reindeers – could've finished off by confessin' my secret passion for a penguin. (*Genuine laughter from all of them.* PRESLEY *waves as if 'goodbye' to an audience.*)

'Well, goodnight and God bless, folks, from Elvis the Pelvis, the penguin-sniffer.' (*Stops – despite the enjoyment.*) What does 'propensity' mean?

MARTY: *Well* . . . er, why?

OLDER PRESLEY: I just remembered it. 'Passion' an' 'penguins' must have brought it on. 'Propensity'. It's a word. I've heard it. Maybe I read it. (*Looks slyly at them.*) Could be someone said it about me, now that I recall. Maybe one of them New York writers. Some interview I did last year – man was a smart-ass – kept on usin' big words – like 'Connecticut'. Yeah, went back to the big city an' wrote all that clever snide stuff. Said I had a . . . propensity for good an' evil. Think it must have been after I kicked his ass down the stairs – but I believe I do. Kinda like that, you know, the twin forces of good an' evil an' which one's goin' to win the war; should be a movie – (*Laughs.*) But what does 'propensity' *mean*: Exactly? We gotta dictionary anywhere?

MARTY: Gotta Bible. Got hundreds of them.

OLDER PRESLEY: Not the same – someone get me a dictionary.
(JO JO *and* MARTY *look at each other. Both go to rise and go.* MARTY *beats* JO JO *to it.* JO JO *scowls and looks away – enough is enough.* PRESLEY *points out, then looks to* JO JO.)
Give me 'sixty-eight, man. Some Christmas that was!

JO JO: (*Into intercom*) 'Sixty-eight. Christmas.
(*The black-leather* YOUNGER PRESLEY *in silhouette, behind and above them.*)

OLDER PRESLEY: Hey – hey baby – (*puts his arm around her*) – don't laugh when I ask you this – but did you ever see anyone so beautiful in all your life – oh look at that . . . just look at that. Everythin' I ever did out there in the . . . world – all summed up that night. Wish everythin' else was so simple.
(*As he speaks, the lights dim down on the scene, leaving a spotlight that focuses on the* OLDER PRESLEY *and* REDHEAD.)

Christmas Spectacular. 1968.
The lights come up on a replica of part of the Presley Christmas spectacular of 1968. The YOUNGER PRESLEY *and the boys in the band, including* GERRY, DUKE, MARTY *and* JO JO (*if* JO JO *can run fast*). *The* YOUNGER PRESLEY *in strutting black leather, still laughing. The table is again used as the stage. The* YOUNGER PRESLEY *has just completed 'Blue Christmas' to great applause. He is in a corner of a square-shaped stage (surrounded in the show by a cluster of* FANS). *His* 'MEN' *are close to him, but not at his height.*

He is the undoubted focus. He sits on a stool, guitar in hand.

YOUNGER PRESLEY: We, er, I think I'll put a strap on this and stand up.

(*He looks around – no strap. Laughter from* ONE OF HIS MEN *just manages to undercut a flash of anger from* PRESLEY.)

No strap.

MARTY: (*To the tune of 'One Night':*) 'No strap for you – '

YOUNGER PRESLEY:

Is what I'm now looking for.

(*The music starts as* PRESLEY *taps out the rhythm. He stands and busks, strapless.*)

The things I did in that song

Would make the dream . . .

Where – where's the strap?

(ONE OF HIS MEN *lifts a microphone and stands up to him. They go into 'One Night' like this.*)

Always lived fairly quiet life,

But now I know that very quiet life

Been too lonely, I said, too long.

One night with you

Is what I'm now planning for,

The things that we two could plan

Would make my dreams come true.

Always lived a fairly quite life,

I ain't never did no wrong,

Now I know that very quiet life

Been too lonely far too long.

One night with you

Is what I'm now planning for,

The things that we two could plan

Would make the earth stand still.

Always lived a very quiet life

(*Laughs.*)

I ain't never did no wrong,

(*Looks to the others and grins.*)

Now I know that very quiet life

Been too lonely too long.

60

One night with you
Is what I'm now planning for,
The things that we two could plan
Would make my dreams come true!
(*He goes straight into 'All Shook Up'.*)
Well, bless my soul, what's wrong with me,
I'm itching like a man on a fuzzy tree,
My friends say I'm acting wild as a bug,
I'm in love, I'm all shook up,
Well, my hands are shakin', my knees are weak,
I can't seem to stand on my own two feet,
What do you think when you have such luck,
I'm all shook up,
Well, please don't ask me what's on my mind,
I'm a little mixed up, but I'm feelin' fine,
When I'm near the girl that I love best,
My heart beats so, it scares me to death,
Well, she touch my hand, what a chill I got,
Her lips are live, a volcano is hot,
I'm proud to say that she's my buttercup,
I'm in love, I'm all shook up,
My tongue gets tired when I try to speak,
My insides shake like a leaf on a tree,
There's only one cure for this body of mine,
And that's to have that girl that I love so fine,
She touch my hand, what a chill I got,
Her lips are live, a volcano is hot,
I'm proud to say that she's my buttercup,
I'm in love, I'm all shook up.

Gracelands. The viewing room.
The OLDER PRESLEY *sitting there, head turned away. He is*
quietly *sobbing. Perhaps some of the tears are tears of joy – perhaps*
REDHEAD *is holding him, tight.* JO JO *stares out.* MARTY *stands*
there with a dictionary in his hands.
MARTY and REDHEAD: 'Memories . . . memories . . .
    sweetened through the ages just like wine . . .'
OLDER PRESLEY: Oh really?

REDHEAD: You were wonderful, Elvis.
(*She smiles but he is not laughing.*)
Oh honey, come on, you done good but let's just call it a
. . . night. Let's –
(PRESLEY *stands up, points out.*)
OLDER PRESLEY: You – you – *you*. Why you – *me*. What . . . I
mean, how . . . someone had to tell me – said to – I dunno
who it was – said – I'd done a couple of concerts – musta
been 'fifty-four – said: 'What in God's name's goin' on,
man, what're those little girls screamin' at me for?' Said:
'It's your left leg, Elvis, that left leg.' I said: 'What? What
left . . . ?' (*Moves his left leg in the manner of the* YOUNGER
PRESLEY.) Oh that left leg! That left leg – got me into this
. . . this mess. Of blues . . . I mean, Reds – am I
ungrateful or what? Had a life like nobody else ever had –
nobody. Could've been a 42-year-old truck driver now –
highpoint of my life leadin' a convoy through Dayton,
Ohio, crashin' through a road block doin' 95 . . . done
everythin' – means nothin'. NOTHIN'!
(*He sits down heavily, looks briefly to the others.* JO JO *looks
down.* MARTY *comes to the rescue.*)
MARTY: Anyway, got that 'propensity' word, boss. See – means
'a natural disposition'.
OLDER PRESLEY: (*Dragging himself up*) Yeah . . . 'A natural
disposition for good an' evil' . . . *Yeah* . . . but what does
'disposition' mean?
(*We are aware before* MARTY *that despite the state he has just
been in,* PRESLEY *is sending* MARTY *up.* MARTY *looks down
at the dictionary, begins to look for 'disposition', then glances
back at the smiling* PRESLEY.)
It's all right, man, I know what 'disposition' means . . .
that's me an' Jesse, y' see, twin forces of good an' evil – tell
you what, if that boy'd have lived, he'd have been one evil
son of a bitch . . . (*Kicks out gently at the other throne, spins it
around.*) *You* would have won, you mother, you would have
been bad enough to win . . . bad enough.
MARTY: (*Quickly*) All right, on with the show – what's next?
What we got left in the vaults, Jo Jo?

JO JO: (*Shrugs.*) Not a lot – got Hawaii.
(PRESLEY *looks at him.*)

MARTY: Hey – world-wide – world records again, boss. Two hundred and fifty million viewers – some audience – like to see that again.

OLDER PRESLEY: Hawaii?

JO JO: Yeah. It's there.

OLDER PRESLEY: It was just after me an' Cilla an' all that.

JO JO: No, it wasn't.
(PRESLEY *glares at him.*)
Coupla years f'Christ's sake . . . Yeah, all right, it was just after Cilla. (*Turns away, talks to himself.*) An' the moons a balloon . . .

OLDER PRESLEY: Don't wanna see Hawaii. I was fat. An' Priscilla had gone.

REDHEAD: Let's not see Hawaii then, honey, I don't mind. (*Kisses him.*) An' you were never fat.

OLDER PRESLEY: (*Glances at her.*) It's all right, Reds. I can cope with that now. Took my mama. I can take my wife.
(*He stands up with sudden resolution, takes his guitar.*
REDHEAD *puts her head in her hands and turns completely away.* MARTY *climbs up with him, to give him support and perhaps some basic backing.* JO JO *deliberately stays where he is, looking away.*)
My song this, boys, no one else's, my song, try an' take this one away from me . . .
(*He starts singing 'You Gave Me a Mountain This Time' – aggressive.*)
> Born in the heat of the desert,
> My brother died giving me life,
> Deprived of the love of a father,
> Blamed for the loss of his wife,
> You know, Lord, I've been in a prison
> For something I never done,
> It's been one hill after another,
> And I've climbed them all one by one,
> Oh but this time, Lord, you gave me a mountain,
> A mountain I may never climb.

63

> My woman got tired of the heartache,
> Got tired of the grief and the strife,
> So tired of waiting for nothing,
> Just tired of being my wife,
> She took my one ray of sunshine,
> She took my pride and my joy,
> She took my reason for living,
> She took my small baby boy . . .

(*Stumbles to a stop.*)

No, she didn't. She took my small baby girl . . . but ain't nothin' rhymes with 'girl'. 'Cept 'hurl' and 'whirl'. And 'Burl' . . . Ives.

MARTY: (*Desperately*) 'Curl', Elvis.

OLDER PRESLEY: Uh-huh. (*Curls his lip.*) Yeah, 'curl'.

(*Laughs lightly and starts to sing again.*)

> She took my one ray of sunshine,
> She took my pride and my curl,
> She took my reason for living,
> She took my small baby girl . . .

(*Stops again, the guitar dropped to his side.*)

'My reason for living . . .' Yeah. (*Flatly*) 'But this time, Lord, you gave me a mountain, a mountain I may never climb . . .' An' that's what I'm afraid of. Never forget that day, man, an' neither will Duke and Gerry . . . Jo Jo's right, those boys better come back . . . (*Reaches out for a sachet of powder and the bag.*) Just goin' t' the john.

MARTY: I'll er come with you, chief.

OLDER PRESLEY: (*Slight edge*) I can do it on my own, Marty. I learned at a very early age.

MARTY: No, I need a –

OLDER PRESLEY: There's fourteen bathrooms here, boy, find your own.

(*He goes off.*)

JO JO: Still gonna follow him?

MARTY: Come on, man, y' *never* follow him when he looks at you like that.

REDHEAD: (*Standing*) You been jumpin' too long. You jump for

peanuts easy enough – why don't you jump when it's
important?

(*She leaves.* MARTY *whistles.* JO JO *slaps his wrist.*)

MARTY: Consider yourself reprimanded.

JO JO: Think he's comin' back?

MARTY: (*standing*) Was he here in the first place?

(BOTH MEN *go off.*)

DUKE *and* GERRY *and the* ENGLISHMAN.

DUKE: Well, he wasn't around. Simple as that. When the
tomcat's away . . .

ENGLISHMAN: What was he doin'?

DUKE: Tourin'. And whorin'.

GERRY: Boy, was he whorin'!

DUKE: We all were. All got our fair share; secondhand roses, the
little ladies who never quite made the grade with Elvis –
made the grade with us. We weren't *that* particular. I'm
tellin' you, when we got to Vegas – there'd be more women
queuin' outside our rooms than watchin' the show.

(GERRY *smiles in memory and at the exaggeration.*)

Some nights, why, I must've had ten to a dozen, regular,
tricks too, the whole repertoire, walk in the room an' start
climbin' up the closet, all the dirty business in the world
. . . some of those nights, some of those women, the head
they could give . . .

(DUKE *sighs.* GERRY *leans across to the* ENGLISHMAN.)

GERRY: You see, Duke's very heavily into oral sex – yeah, he
never stops talkin' about it for hours.

(*Even* DUKE *laughs.*)

ENGLISHMAN: So, the cat's away –

DUKE: Cilla's out playin'.

(*The* ENGLISHMAN *picks up the piece of paper.*)

ENGLISHMAN: With Mike Stone?

Spring 1973.

The OLDER PRESLEY *in a demented rage, the words and mantra
frenzied.* MARTY *approaches him, followed by* JO JO, *and finally*
DUKE *and* GERRY.

OLDER PRESLEY: Mike Stone must die, Mike Stone must die, Mike Stone must die, Mike Stone must die, Mike Stone must die, Mike Stone must die, Mike Stone must die, Mike Stone must die, Mike Stone must die.

(*Finally* DUKE *approaches* PRESLEY, *moves around to face him, both men on their knees.*)

DUKE: Boss –

OLDER PRESLEY: Mike Stone must die, Mike Stone must die, Mike Stone must die, Mike Stone must die – what?

DUKE: Cilla's outside.

OLDER PRESLEY: (*Almost childlike*) My Cilla came back?

DUKE: (*Flatly*) Yeah. We brought her back.

OLDER PRESLEY: (*Childlike*) But Mike Stone must die.

DUKE: I know that – it's been arranged.

OLDER PRESLEY: Mike Stone's gonna die.

DUKE: Free of charge. The Mafia will do it as a favour. For all the pleasure you've given them over the years.

OLDER PRESLEY: Did you hear that – Jesus Christ, that's really . . . nice of them.

(*This time the irony is lost on him, but not, quietly, on the* OTHERS.)

When's it gonna be – when's Mike Stone gonna die?

DUKE: The matter's in hand, Elvis, they've sent two of their best out.

OLDER PRESLEY: They've already gone . . . to kill Mike Stone?

DUKE: (*Nods.*) Violin cases and piano wire – probably lookin' for a nice big bridge an' some concrete right now.

JO JO: You do know what you're doing', don't you, boss?

(PRESLEY *looks at him.* JO JO *shrugs.*)

Man's gonna die.

OLDER PRESLEY: I'm the King. If presidents an' godfathers can order a man's death – so can a king. An' Mike Stone must die, Mike Stone must die.

DUKE: (*Matter of fact*) He's going to. Wanna see Cilla now?

OLDER PRESLEY: Yeah. See my little Cilla . . . The Killer an' Cilla.

(PRESLEY *rises to his full height – and strut. Takes hold of* DUKE *by the shoulders, like a godfather without kisses.*)

66

Tell y', Duke – that's what I call takin' care of business, man . . . Send my woman in to me . . .

(*He stands there waiting as the others go off, back turned to where* PRISCILLA *will make her entry. Moody and mean, one shoulder up, one shoulder down. Wow . . .* PRISCILLA *enters.* DUKE *leaves. She sees* PRESLEY. *Despite being nervous, she still manages a half-smile at his adopted pose. She comes up to and past him, turns and faces him.*)

OLDER PRESLEY: Ah. Hi! You came.

PRISCILLA: I had no option.

OLDER PRESLEY: You lied to me.

PRISCILLA: I . . . had no option.

OLDER PRESLEY: Christ – what is this – a new version of the Fifth Amendment – 'I had no option'? You ran off with Mike Stone – 'I had no option.' You humped the ass off him – 'I had no option' – *You won't let me see Lisa Marie* – 'I had – '

PRISCILLA: All right, I lied to you – and are you going to stand there and tell me you didn't lie to me?

OLDER PRESLEY: My friend, my so-called friend – (*stumbles over saying it*) – M-Mike Stone. Behind my back.

PRISCILLA: How could it be behind your back when you were never there? To have your back turned.

OLDER PRESLEY: I was tourin'.

PRISCILLA: For two years? (*Pause.*) How many other women did *you* have in those two years?

OLDER PRESLEY: (*Flaring*) Hundreds, babe, goddamn hundreds – thousands even! Everyone – everywhere. No woman *ever* said no to me – *nobody* says no to me. I'm Elvis Presley. And I want you back here.

PRISCILLA: No.

OLDER PRESLEY: And I want my daughter. Cilla, I want my daughter. I'm her daddy. (*Suddenly*) I'll break every goddamn bone in your lousy body if I can't have my sweet little baby.

PRISCILLA: If you're in a fit state, you can see her whenever –

OLDER PRESLEY: I DON'T WANNA SEE HER – I WANT HER. You can't take her away.

PRISCILLA: Why can't we settle this like sane grown-up people?

OLDER PRESLEY: (*Like a mad child*) You took my baby away from me – you went off in the night like a cheap one-trick whore with my friend – you made a fool of me – and you're gonna pay – he's gonna pay – every sucker involved's gonna pay – an' then I'll have my Lisa Marie back where she belongs. Cos . . . cos I know, I've been told, you – you have my little baby girl sleeping in the same room as you an' Mike Stone. There – there – at the side of the bed when you're . . . you're –

PRISCILLA: It's not true.

OLDER PRESLEY: There in the same room.

PRISCILLA: (*Quietly*) I swear to you, that's just not true.

OLDER PRESLEY: But you won't be doing it much longer. (*Looks away from her.*)

PRISCILLA: Mike's already scared of that.

OLDER PRESLEY: He better be. (*Shrugs.*) Scared of what, anyway?

PRISCILLA: Nothing bad is going to happen to Mike, baby.

OLDER PRESLEY: Y' mean not ever? Immortality as well? Some man this boy must be.

PRISCILLA: You know what I mean.

OLDER PRESLEY: Y' wrong, Cilla. If I want to, I can do anything.

PRISCILLA: But you won't want to.

OLDER PRESLEY: Oh. And why won't I?

PRISCILLA: Cos if you do, I'll make sure you never see Lisa Marie ever again.
(*A very long pause.* PRESLEY *goes from murder to tears as, finally, the little boy speaks.*)

OLDER PRESLEY: Oh baby . . . Oh Cilla baby . . . how much more loss can I . . . ? I don't want to lose Lisa Marie as well, that's why I . . . I done . . . things. But I'll do anything you want, Cilla. An' . . . an' I won't ever do anything you don't want me to do. (*Shakes his head resolutely.*) Please, sweetheart . . . Why . . . why you go away? I gave you everythin'. I don't understand . . . why you go?

68

PRISCILLA: (*Gently*) You gave me everything money could buy. But you never gave me time. And I had a lot of time. On my hands. So in that time . . . I grew up.

OLDER PRESLEY: (*Still not listening*) You had money, you had cars, you had – you went to that finishing school, I paid for that – you studied ballet an' things – all those clothes – I was good to you and – you did that design course – I was good to you, and I've been good to Lisa Marie –

PRISCILLA: (*Coming closer to him*) You were a wonderful husband and the best daddy in the whole world. When you were there. But you were never there.

OLDER PRESLEY: I'll change, I'll – I can – won't do nothin' without you – wanna play the drums in the show? (*With desperate charm*) Hey – hey! You could do that bit at the end of the show – (*Adopts a deep gruff voice:*) 'Ladies and gentlemen, Elvis has left the building.' Be a duo – yeah – a duo – like Johnny Cash an' Rosalyn Carter, except better lookin'. Clean my teeth, Cilla, you'll be there – baby, walk the dog, I'll be right by your side, ballet lessons . . . (*Half-heartedly lifts his leg into a ballet position, lets his leg fall, and then his head.*) Mike Stone good to you?

PRISCILLA: Yes.

OLDER PRESLEY: Treats you well? With . . . you know, dignity?

PRISCILLA: Yes yes. (*Smiles.*) With dignity. But he's not you.

OLDER PRESLEY: What . . . do you mean?

PRISCILLA: Everyone wants you. No one really wants Mike Stone . . . 'cept me.

OLDER PRESLEY: I love you, Cilla. I love you. You should thank God I love you. Cos I don't want anythin' to happen to spoil – hurt – trouble – no trouble – you want anything – just call me. See the lawyers – tell them what you want . . . What do you want?

PRISCILLA: Nothing. I just want to go now. Please.

(PRESLEY *nods, holds his arms out. She goes to him. He puts his arms around her.*)

OLDER PRESLEY: I'm going to make you so happy – you wait and see – you an' little Lisa Marie – gonna be the two happiest people ever lived.

PRISCILLA: Just . . . just leave Mike alone, please, Elvis, it was nothin' to do with you and –
(PRESLEY *has already left her arms – in sudden panic. He moves away from her rapidly.*)

OLDER PRESLEY: Yeah yeah – you go honey – I'll call you tonight – we'll have one of those lovin' little talks like we used to – gonna be – I've gotta – go.
(*He moves away very quickly. She is bewildered, but going.*)

The YOUNGER PRESLEY *sings 'I Was the One'.*

YOUNGER PRESLEY:
> I was the one who taught her to kiss,
> The way that she kisses you now,
> And you know the way she touches your cheek,
> Well, I taught her how.
>
> I was the one who taught her to cry,
> When she wants you under her spell,
> The sight of her tears drives you out of your mind,
> I taught her so well.
>
> And then one day I had my love as perfect as could be,
> She lived, she loved, she laughed, she cried,
> And it was all for me.
>
> I'll never know who taught her to lie,
> And now that it's over and done,
> Well, who learnt a lesson when she broke my heart?
> I was the one.

Simultaneous: Gracelands. 1973.

MARTY *and* JO JO, DUKE *and* GERRY, *and a demented* OLDER PRESLEY, *kneeling in another near-mantra, as he writes furiously on a piece of paper.*

OLDER PRESLEY: Mike Stone must not die, Mike Stone must not die – *Mike Stone must not die!* (*To* DUKE) Come on, man, take care of business – Mike Stone must not die.
(DUKE *and the* OTHERS *exchange glances of incomprehension.*

DUKE *is already beginning to dial a number, phone book open. He will dial and dial again as* PRESLEY *talks and writes.*)

I promise never to to anything terrible like this again, I promise never to harbour violent thoughts like these again, I promise never to hurt in any way shape or form my Priscilla, I promise to look after my little Lisa Marie all my life, I promise never to try and get Mike Stone killed ever ever again, I promise, I promise, I hereby promise. I swear to God on everything I hold sacred. (*Stops writing, looks up at the* OTHERS.) Mike Stone must not die.

(DUKE *starts dialling even faster.* PRESLEY *pushes the paper away.*)

Someone put that away. Put it somewhere safe, if I ever get like this again, show it to me, don't ever let me forget . . . *I'm not a bad man* . . . come on, someone take this.

(DUKE *stops phoning, slides the paper towards himself, pockets it as he puts his arm around* PRESLEY *and leads him out.*)

'I Was the One' *is completed by the* YOUNGER PRESLEY.

DUKE *and* GERRY *and the* ENGLISHMAN.

DUKE: Never made so many phone calls in one night. Elvis sitting there chantin' 'Mike Stone must not die' over and over again . . . Got to the stage I was just ringin' people up with Italian names – 'sorry to bother you, Mr Pagioni, you're not a member of the Mafia by any chance, are you?' Finally pulled the two hit men off. Know where they were? In an apartment buildin' overlookin' Mike Stone's place. Don't that just send a chill right down your spine?

ENGLISHMAN: Why did you do it?

DUKE: (*Cold*) Cos Elvis told me to get it done.

ENGLISHMAN: Even though it was . . . cold-blooded murder?

DUKE: Wasn't cold-blooded, friend. Blood was boilin' over.

ENGLISHMAN: But didn't someone try to reason with him?

GERRY: Yeah. We all did.

DUKE: Can't reason with a 'god'. Not when a 'god' gets like that.

GERRY: Just got to take care of business – hope he comes to his senses.

DUKE: And he did.

ENGLISHMAN: Only just.

DUKE: Can't we talk about the weather? You English like talkin' about that, don't you? Cats an' dogs an' all that. Awfully awfully.

ENGLISHMAN: But if Elvis had said, 'Carry on – Mike Stone must die' – he'd have been killed?

(DUKE *flicks off the tape recorder*.)

DUKE: Yeah . . . (*Leans forward, grabs hold of the* ENGLISHMAN *by the shirt*.) But if you ever print that – remember this – I still got the name an' address of the local godfather. (*Lets go and leans back, looks towards the phone*.) Quarter before one – give him till one – and then I'm going over there to see him – and then I'll get *everythin'* you need. *I'm* takin' care of business.

(*The lights go down on them*.)

Gracelands. The viewing room.

The OLDER PRESLEY *has not moved. Nobody has moved.*

OLDER PRESLEY: Go to bed. You all go to bed. Wanna be on my own.

REDHEAD: Wouldn't it be wiser if we all go to bed?

OLDER PRESLEY: I want to be on my own. (*Smiles gently*.) Four in a bed ain't bein' alone. It's somethin' else altogether. Go on, hurry along. Children. Check on Lisa Marie for me, sweetheart. (*Puts his hand to the side of her face*.) I'm nearly finished now . . . down here.

(*She kisses him lightly on the cheek, leaves.* MARTY *and* JO JO *aren't going to argue – especially* JO JO.)

Night, Marty.

MARTY: Night, boss.

OLDER PRESLEY: Night, Jo Jo.

JO JO: Yeah. Night.

OLDER PRESLEY: See you in the mornin'. *Jo Jo*.

JO JO: (*Not looking*) Night.

OLDER PRESLEY: Night, boys . . . sweet dreams.

(*He sighs very quietly. The phone rings. He picks it up*.)

Daddy . . . Don't wanna talk to you now, Daddy. It's too late . . . An' I don't wanna talk no money! Daddy get off the phone . . . yeah yeah, well listen, tell the Colonel to shove it.

(*He drops the phone down, puts his head down. Then picks up the phone, dials impatiently.*)

Come on, come on, you dumb stupid – ah hi honey, got a sudden urge to see your peach melbas. (*Laughs.*) And your pancakes in syrup, not to mention your banana boats. But most of all, I'd give anythin' for a glimpse of your doughnuts. (*Whistles.*) Covered in honey an' treacle, an' standin' alongside a couple of tubs of ice cream . . . Well, I wanted them ten minutes ago, Marie-Anne, so y' already late in deliverin' . . .

(*He puts the phone down. Picks up the piece of paper again, puts it down. Picks up his guitar, holds it in his lap. Brings the attaché case towards himself, flicks it open. Looks at the contents, takes a couple of loose tablets out, looks at them, flicks them up in the air like a child would with a Smartie, tries to catch them in his mouth. Repeats again with the next tablet. Begins to play 'I'm So Lonesome I Could Cry' on guitar, whistles the tune. While* PRESLEY *sits at his table,* MARTY *and* JO JO *trudge towards their rooms.* MARTY *is a little way ahead of* JO JO.)

JO JO: Marty . . .

(MARTY *stops.*)

Listen, man, I'm goin'.

MARTY: Goin' where?

JO JO: Off into the night. As they say. Get my things together and go. I just can't take . . .

MARTY: I know. I know.

JO JO: Peace of mind, that's all – no more 'Takin' Care of Business', an' takin' care of him.

MARTY: You gonna write a book too?

JO JO: Had offers.

MARTY: Haven't we all?

JO JO: Some Englishman a couple of months ago – sniffin' around – talkin' a lot of money.

MARTY: For the dirt.

JO JO: Or the truth. After all, I was there too that night with Cilla. And the rest. (*Sees the contempt on* MARTY's *face.*) I know, I know, look, I'm just goin', all right? Nothin' more. For the time bein'. See what happens. Why don't you come with me? You've been with him since 'fifty-six – you've got a tale to tell.

MARTY: Nah. Not me. Not yet. Maybe never . . .
(*They embrace briefly, go to turn away.*)
What shall I tell the Boss?

JO JO: Tell him I still love him but I'm a married man.
(*They go off. The* OLDER PRESLEY *stops playing and whistling, eyelids drooping.*)

OLDER PRESLEY: Stay here with me, Jesse, don't go now – too many other ghosts for you to go now . . .
(DUKE *is standing to his side, wearing a jacket.*)
Duke.

DUKE: How's it goin', man?

OLDER PRESLEY: Been thinkin' about you.

DUKE: (*Looks around.*) On y' own?

OLDER PRESLEY: (*Trying to come up, not go down.*) It's all right, no, it's all right, times when a man needs to be alone – just sat here singin', playin' this old Gibson I found, rootin' around in the back of the house. Got your message – sounded sort of promisin', Duke . . .
(*Silence.*)
Glad you came over. We can talk properly . . . Now.

DUKE: So what do you want?

OLDER PRESLEY: Just to talk, man. Talk. In a better way than before . . . Got the impression that you might want to come back . . . You wanna come back?

DUKE: Don't know, man. Really don't know.

OLDER PRESLEY: Yeah . . . Wanted to talk about the good old days . . . glory days . . . when we had a good time. Those times've gone, man. You know, like the song – 'Let the Good Times Roll' – they've rolled away.

DUKE: You pushed them – that's why they rolled.
(PRESLEY *can stand to be humble for only so long.*)

OLDER PRESLEY: They rolled because you were rippin' me off. YOU!

DUKE: Listen, El, if you want the truth – cos it's too late now to bother with lies –

OLDER PRESLEY: What d'you mean – 'It's too late'?

DUKE: Cos there's still a lot of distance between us. 'S all. But the truth is – everyone was rippin' you off – everyone always has – an' none more so than you yourself – so don't give me all that crap.
(*A brief silence.*)
Come on, man – what did *we* do – in comparison with all the other creeps who hang around you – still. Who loves you, baby – *who*? You don't know.

OLDER PRESLEY: (*Singing, trying for irony*) 'You don't know the one who cries at night . . . You give your hand to me and then you say goodbye . . .'

DUKE: You said goodbye. Or rather, you went away and got your daddy to say goodbye.

OLDER PRESLEY: I didn't want you to go – it was . . . money and stuff. Colonel.

DUKE: But when the time came to say goodbye, you couldn't even do it yourself. After twenty-four years.

OLDER PRESLEY: (*Little boy, genuinely*) I'm sorry.

DUKE: That's not a reason. Give me a reason.

OLDER PRESLEY: Somethin' had to go – we had overheads, expenses – I was losin' money – that crazy volleyball project – remember that – you know how much they took me for – million three hundred thousand. US dollars. For two goddamn volleyball courts – an' I don't even like volleyball that much. Asked me for a hundred grand once – a hundred grand. I asked what it was for – said for an accountant. Jesus Christ, what kind of a union them accountants got?

DUKE: Why didn't you do to them what you did to us, Elvis? Get your daddy to put his arm around *them* an' give them a week's notice – a week's notice. Maybe we need a union.

OLDER PRESLEY: (*Quietly*) You won't need for nothing . . . when you write your book. If you write that book. If it's

75

that kind of book.

DUKE: It'll be a true book. That's all.

OLDER PRESLEY: Well, I'm dead then, may as well go now.

DUKE: Go where?

OLDER PRESLEY: Oh just go.

DUKE: It'll only be the kind of things people are interested in.

OLDER PRESLEY: Huh. People are interested in shit an' filth. If I heard that Burt Reynolds was a transvestite junkie, I'd be interested.

DUKE: Some people might sort of consider you . . . had a drugs problem, man.

OLDER PRESLEY: *You can't lay that one on me* – I only take prescribed medicine. I only take prescribed medicine. You hear that? For my condition.

DUKE: It must be a bad condition, man, cos it's a hell of a big list.

OLDER PRESLEY: I'm not a junkie – I hate junkies an' pushers an' dope dealers – you know that – President Nixon made me a Special Agent for the Bureau of Narcotics and Dangerous Drugs – that's how much I hate them – the President himself – you were there in the goddamn Oval Office. Nixon was smashed – but I ain't no junkie!
(*He looks down at his attaché case, slams it shut.*)

DUKE: (*Easily*) All right all right, you just take a hell of a lot of medicine. Forget it. Listin' the medicine'll do. Might take up a couple of pages but –

OLDER PRESLEY: You ain't got no proof.

DUKE: You were hidin' away when we left, Elvis – remember – you don't know what we took with us. An' what we got. What we already had.

OLDER PRESLEY: I know one thing you got.

DUKE: Oh yeah? What's that?

OLDER PRESLEY: You know. I gave it to you. Concerning Priscilla.

DUKE: Well, that was when you really began to hit the . . . medicine. When Cilla went.

OLDER PRESLEY: No. It's more than that. And you know it. Come on, you got the note. I gave it to you. (*Smiles bitterly.*)

76

For 'safe keeping' . . . It's been on my mind. That note.

DUKE: You mean the note sayin' you'll – what was it? – 'never threaten Mike Stone's life again'. Y' mean that one?

OLDER PRESLEY: Yeah. Gonna put that in your book as well? (DUKE *shrugs.* PRESLEY *hardly focuses on him.*) I was disturbed . . . upset. Man can do all kinds of things when he's in that state – particularly if he's allowed to . . . do all kinds of things.

DUKE: It was still a crazy thing to do though, wasn't it? Gettin' the Mafia to kill Mike Stone.

OLDER PRESLEY: (*Not listening*) You can't tell the . . . truth, not if you love me.

DUKE: I love my wife an' kids – I'd like them to live in a house again.

OLDER PRESLEY: Yeah . . . (*Realizes.*) *You sold your house?*

DUKE: Week's notice doesn't pay the bills for long, man. You wanna try an' live outside of Gracelands sometime, Elvis. Go somewhere *real* – anywhere'll do – you'll get a shock.

OLDER PRESLEY: (*Meaning it, as only he can*) Listen, I wanna make it up to you – a man's family must never – shit, I didn't mean to hurt your family – whatever you want, Duke, Gerry too – just . . . don't tell the truth. Not all that stuff. That's the kind of truth that hurts.

DUKE: You said it.

OLDER PRESLEY: I did good things as well. (*He opens the attaché case, will begin to take some tablets.*)

DUKE: I know you did – everyone knows that – good things – great things.

OLDER PRESLEY: You'll destroy me.

DUKE: Look in the mirror when you say that. Don't accuse me.

OLDER PRESLEY: Well, I'm not destroyed, I'm not, I've got my health –

DUKE: Since when?

OLDER PRESLEY: I'm all right now, I've been scared, yeah, I had some kind of blockage – but it's all fine – I had a medical – best doctors, full works, I thought I was going to have to have surgery but I don't – 100 per cent A1 all right – so you can't say that about me – I've got my health, I've got my little daughter, I can still sing, man, ten thousand people a night can't all be wrong, been thinkin' about gettin' married again, I've got a lot to live for. I'm one happy man.

DUKE: Pleased to hear it.

OLDER PRESLEY: I bet you are – not goin' to go under because of you, you know.

DUKE: Whatever we write. About whatever happened.

OLDER PRESLEY: I ain't gonna plead, man. You do what you have to do, and I'll just take care of business.

DUKE: That a threat?

OLDER PRESLEY: Doesn't matter what it is – you won't hurt me – no one'll believe you – not about me.

DUKE: Not even with evidence. In writing.

OLDER PRESLEY: (*Flaring*) Don't *you* taunt *me*, man – cos the world'll laugh in your face – and hey – not only that, but every man who ever lost his woman'll wish he could have hired the Mafia free of charge – Mike Stone's only alive now out of the kindness of my heart – that's *power* for you – even in so-called defeat. And I'm warnin' you, I'll have your balls if you say anything bad about me in that book! I'm the King. I'm still the King.

(DUKE *smiles warmly, disarmingly*.)

DUKE: Ever thought you might be a Greek god?

OLDER PRESLEY: A what?

DUKE: A Greek god.

OLDER PRESLEY: You pullin' my pisser?

(DUKE *smiles again*.)

You're not comin' back, are you?

DUKE: No.

OLDER PRESLEY: All right. OK. Fine. I hope it works out for you. I really do. You take care now, give my love to Suzanne and the family – love your family, Duke, and look after them. I wish I was as lucky as you.

DUKE: . . . I wish I was Elvis Presley.

(PRESLEY *laughs*. DUKE *shakes his head*.)

OLDER PRESLEY: Well, if you're gonna go, go now, or else you've got to stay all night!

78

(*He laughs again.* DUKE *doesn't – he would like to stay all night.*)

Cos I feel like playin' some more music, somethin' good, cos that's how I feel – feel really good right now.

DUKE: I'm glad.

OLDER PRESLEY: I am too. Glad we talked, man – all right – let's leave it at that – I'll always be here, you know that, don't you – just call my name, boy . . . like you always did before. (*Laughs.*) Just remember this, Duke – 'asshole'!

DUKE: Right.

OLDER PRESLEY: Right.

(DUKE *leaves.* PRESLEY *looks desperately towards the other chair.*)

Well . . . that's it then, Jesse, I'm fucked . . . reckon you could have done better – huh? Wanna change places? (*Motions with his hand as if offering to change places.*) Feel like that Black Knight in *Monty Python and the Holy Grail*. Them Monty Python, Jesse, I'm not kiddin', man, they'd have made you laugh – tell y', I love 'em – they're mad – mad as the world outside – that scene in *The Holy Grail*, Christ, when the tall one gets cut up – he was a knight – coulda been a king one day – brave as a bull, he was – but he got cut up – arms and legs an' everythin' – sliced into little bits – an' he still kept goin' – got one leg left – still threatenin' to kick everyone to death – still kept fightin', man – ended up with just his head left in the mud, shoutin', 'Come here, you cowards, I'll bite your ankles . . .' *Kept goin'. Gotta keep goin'.* (*Punches the table top.*)

The room where the ENGLISHMAN, DUKE *and* GERRY *are.*
DUKE *flatly opens up and takes off his jacket, to reveal that he has been wired for sound. Expressionless, he holds his thumb and forefinger together – got it.* DUKE *presses 'play' on the tape. We hear*
OLDER PRESLEY *and* DUKE:

DUKE: It was still a crazy thing to do though, wasn't it, gettin' the Mafia to kill Mike Stone?

OLDER PRESLEY: You can't tell the . . . truth, not if you love me.

ENGLISHMAN: (*Fortunately flatly*) You are going to make an
    awful lot of money, gentlemen. Without any shadow of
    doubt.
DUKE: What do you want us to do, friend – raise our glasses –
    salute the Queen? Celebrate? (*Spits on the floor.*) Think I'll
    just keep on drinkin' instead.
    (*The lights fade down slowly on them.*)
    That's a subtle hint. If you wanna'nother clue – the bar at
    the corner of Tenth closes at two o'clock – and it's nearly
    quarter to.
    (*The* ENGLISHMAN *leaves them.*)
GERRY: An' none of that champagne piss . . .
    (*The lights fade down on them.*)

COLONEL PARKER *and* VERNON PRESLEY. COLONEL PARKER
is closing every book in front of VERNON PRESLEY, *flipping them
shut while* VERNON PRESLEY *peeps out from behind his fingers.*
COLONEL PARKER *packs the books into his briefcase as he talks.*
COLONEL: Your son an' heir has to be told, Vernon.
VERNON PRESLEY: What d'y' think I do with him – talk about
    the baseball results?
COLONEL: Y' may as well, for what good it does.
VERNON PRESLEY: He's 42 years old, I –
COLONEL: Well, isn't it about time he started actin' like it? The
    boy is bankrupt, Vernon, near as damn it – *an' he has to be
    told.*
    (*He walks away.* VERNON PRESLEY *trudges after him.*)

Gracelands.
OLDER PRESLEY: (*Looking towards Jesse's chair*) All right, all
    right, I'll stand or fall by this, Jesse, an' it's a fact – *I done
    a lot of good things, Jesse, I know I have.* Yeah, done some
    bad stuff . . . but . . . show me a man who's got nothin' to
    be deeply ashamed of – an' all y'll be showin' me is a man
    who never lived. (*The barest smile.*) Sounds just like you,
    brother . . .
    (MARIE-ANNE *enters with a tray of monstrous riches.*)
    All right . . . all right, once upon a time I did think about

80

the possibility of killin' someone – admit it was more than a possibility even – but that 'someone' stole the one I love . . . in my fashion. *She* should have died, glad she didn't, didn't want her to die, but coulda coped if she had, couldn't cope at all when she just went away . . . and left me.

(MARIE-ANNE *doesn't even bother any more to look around for anyone. She listens wide-eyed for a while, then turns around and begins to tiptoe off, like the Ghost of Christmas Past. Until . . .*)

Come here. (*Leans madly yet quiet and with warmth towards the other chair.*) No, come on, here.

(MARIE-ANNE *looks desperately behind her now, returns reluctantly. She is just outside of his field of vision. She thinks that he is not looking at her because he is a king and she is his subject. And also because of the subject matter.*)

Maybe you would have handled it better than me – wouldn't have thrown it all away – but say it happened to you – you virgin you –

(MARIE-ANNE *does not, frankly, know what the fuck is going on.*)

– would you have stood there an' let it happen? Answer me – your love has gone – come on, I know you're there – what would you have done?

MARIE-ANNE: I'da – *I'da cut his fuckin' prick off, boss!*

(PRESLEY *hurls sideways to look at her, almost falling in the process as he stands.*)

OLDER PRESLEY: What the – what . . . you shouldn't do that to me, Marie-Anne.

MARIE-ANNE: *I* shouldn't – (*Points between herself and him.*) I thought you were talkin' to me. Just bringin' your . . . things, that's all. Meltin' fast . . .

(*She lays the tray down before him. He is aware that some explanation is required.*)

OLDER PRESLEY: Bet you were wonderin' what was goin' down there – (*Points to both thrones.*) Thought it was for real.

MARIE-ANNE: (*Shakes her head.*) I just thought it was a conversation . . .

OLDER PRESLEY: Uh-huh. It was a film script. (*Nods.*) Yeah. A
    film I'm plannin'. (*Leans forward.*) Learnin' my lines . . .
    big scene. I'm the hero and – kinda moody an' mean, you
    know . . . big-budget production – Clint Eastwood maybe
    – definitely got Diana Ross –
MARIE-ANNE: Oh yeah – she playin' my part?
OLDER PRESLEY: (*Any diversion*) Well – can't sing as good as
    you, honey – have to dub your voice on after – but the
    good news is you get to sing the title track.
MARIE-ANNE: (*Laughs.*) I wish I could sing.
OLDER PRESLEY: (*In all innocence*) Ah come on, all negros can
    sing.
MARIE-ANNE: (*Easily*) Oh yeah – suppose we can all shine
    shoes, pick cotton an' play basketball. Run the hundred
    yards too.
    (PRESLEY *laughs in acknowledgement.*)
OLDER PRESLEY: Bet I can teach you. Betcha I can. First music
    I ever heard was when I was stuck to my mama's skirt
    listenin' to Gospel.
MARIE-ANNE: I wasn't no different – still flat as a pancake.
    (*They both look down at the pancakes on the tray, smile.*)
    Eat up.
OLDER PRESLEY: Nah – (*Pushes the tray away.*) Rather teach
    you to sing first.
MARIE-ANNE: You'll starve to death then, honey.
OLDER PRESLEY: Tell you what – got just the song for you –
    I'll sing it – you come in second time around. All right?
    (*He begins to sing 'If We Never Meet Again', – almost . . .*)
    Soon we'll come to the end of a lollipop.
    (*They both giggle. He starts again – seriously and continues
    quietly beneath and around the following scene.*)

DUKE *and* GERRY *and the* ENGLISHMAN.
They are slugged in their seats. More bottles – whisky.
DUKE: Nah, you watch – be the biggest thing to happen to Elvis
    since the 'sixty-eight TV special – when they find out what
    he's really been doin' – there'll be thousands out there
    night after night – everyone from Tucson to Tallahassee –

ENGLISHMAN: (*Nodding*) Voyeurs.
GERRY: Where's that?
    (*The* OTHER TWO *stare at him.*)
DUKE: D'you do this on purpose or what, Gerry?
GERRY: Do what?
DUKE: (*Shakes his head.*) Nah, Elvis – the son of a bitch'll
    probably outlive us all – but *they* won't know that – ten
    dollars a time – see if he'll fall down this time – will he get
    up again – could this be the last time . . . doin' him a
    favour really . . .
    (*Silence.*)
ENGLISHMAN: You don't miss anything?
DUKE: To do with him?
ENGLISHMAN: Yes.
DUKE: (*Flatly*) I miss everything. Always will.
GERRY: Yeah.
    (*The lights begin to go down – very slowly.*)
DUKE: The one thing I really miss is knowin' that that man –
    the man'll be there now makin' music, about the only joy
    left for him, but I know I'll never be there again playin'
    that music with him.
GERRY: (*Sighing*) Ahhh shit, don't . . .

Gracelands. The viewing room.

MARIE-ANNE *sings a verse of 'If We Never Meet Again' as the
previous scene finishes. It is passable, and growing in conviction. The*
OLDER PRESLEY *joins in the background vocal. Sitting somewhere
near them, and coming into light and focus when required, will be*
COLONEL PARKER *and* VERNON PRESLEY.
OLDER PRESLEY: If that ain't singin' babe, I'm Zsa Zsa Gabor.
    (*Flicks at his chest.*) You ain't never goin' to play Las Vegas
    but you can sing, you just never been shown. Come on,
    come in behind me on the chorus on this, darlin', nice an'
    deep –
        Soon we'll come to the end of life's journey,
        And perhaps never meet any more,
        Till we gather in the heaven's bright city
        Far away on that beautiful shore.

(PRESLEY *begins the next line.* MARIE-ANNE *echoes the last four words.* PRESLEY *sings the next line. Then* MARIE-ANNE *is joined by the* COLONEL *and* VERNON *in the echo.*)

If we never meet again this side of heaven,

MARIE-ANNE:

. . . this side of heaven,

OLDER PRESLEY:

As we struggle through this world and its trials,

MARIE-ANNE, COLONEL and VERNON PRESLEY:

. . . and all its trials,

OLDER PRESLEY:

There's another –

(*He stops singing, turns around. So does* MARIE-ANNE. COLONEL *and* VERNON PRESLEY *do not. They become a grotesque grinning duo.*)

COLONEL and VERNON PRESLEY:

There's another meeting place somewhere in heaven,

COLONEL:

. . . somewhere in heaven,

COLONEL and VERNON PRESLEY:

By the side of the river of life,

COLONEL:

. . . river of life.

COLONEL and VERNON PRESLEY:

Where the charming roses bloom for ever,

COLONEL:

. . . for ever.

COLONEL and VERNON PRESLEY:

And where separation comes no more.

COLONEL:

. . . never more.

COLONEL and VERNON PRESLEY:

If we never meet again this side of heaven,
We'll meet you on that beautiful shore.

(PRESLEY *stares coldly at them. Casually he turns and motions to* MARIE-ANNE *to come nearer. Even more casually he inspects his hands, selects and takes the biggest ring off a finger, holds it out to* MARIE-ANNE.)

OLDER PRESLEY: Here y' are, honey – (*With the slightest of edges*) And don't say no because a refusal always offends.

MARIE-ANNE: I can't.

OLDER PRESLEY: You can. And you will.

(*She takes it.* VERNON PRESLEY *shakes his head. The* COLONEL *consults his papers.*)

MARIE-ANNE: I never did nothin'.

OLDER PRESLEY: You took me away from where I was headin'. An' I didn't really wanna go there . . .

(*He almost brusquely indicates for her to go. She does.* PRESLEY *approaches the* TWO MEN, *hitching his trousers up in the macho manner often used in his stage performances.*)

Oh hello daddy – fired anyone lately?

VERNON PRESLEY: You know how much that ring cost?

COLONEL: (*Reading the cost from his accounts*) Forty-three thousand five hundred dollars. (*Looks up.*) After discount. Before tax.

OLDER PRESLEY: (*To* VERNON) Is it your ring?

(*No answer. He looks to the* COLONEL.)

Is it yours?

(*No answer.*)

Well, it ain't mine neither. Any more.

(*He moves off the table, stands behind his throne.*)

COLONEL: Hardly anythin's yours any more, Elvis.

OLDER PRESLEY: (*Viciously*) Probably because I give you between 50 and 85 per cent of everythin' I earn, Colonel. Boy, was I stupid. Man, I was so slow, I didn't have a birthmark till I was 29. (*Laughs.*) 'Birthmark'. I gotta birthmark – nobody can see. (*Turns to his* FATHER.) And you, daddy, get that chair back where it belongs, – at the side of mine – or maybe you'll find that firin' people runs in the family.

(VERNON PRESLEY *moves slightly sideways to accommodate the other throne.*)

COLONEL: It isn't me who spends your money, Elvis – it's you.

VERNON PRESLEY: Son –

OLDER PRESLEY: Shut up, daddy. (*Sits down and drags the melting mess on the tray towards him.*) I'm eating.

85

(*Pause.*)

COLONEL: Elvis . . . Elvis, remember 'seventy-four when you earned a million and a half – and spent more than three . . . ?

OLDER PRESLEY: Boy, did I have some fun that year. (*Carries on eating.*)

COLONEL: Well, you must have had an awful lot of fun this year as well. An' it's only August.

OLDER PRESLEY: Yeah. August. (*To* VERNON PRESLEY) Know what happened yesterday, daddy? (*Stops, looks at his watch.*) No, day before yesterday. (*Whistles and shakes his head.*) Real bad.

VERNON PRESLEY: Er no.

OLDER PRESLEY: It was the anniversary of the death of your wife. Daddy. (*Total wild hate all over the* OLDER PRESLEY, *despite furious ice-cream eating.*) Your first wife.

VERNON PRESLEY: I remembered. Just didn't tell you I –

OLDER PRESLEY: Get the fuck out of here.

(VERNON PRESLEY, *bitterly embarrassed, is willing to go.*)

COLONEL: I've been doin' some workin' out, Elvis.

OLDER PRESLEY: You could do with it, Colonel – exercise is very good for you at your age.

COLONEL: In the last ten years, you have given away cars – just cars – not includin' jewellery and houses an' other things – just cars –

OLDER PRESLEY: What is this – *This is Your Life*? All the cars gonna come out from behind the curtains? 'Hi, Elvis, – fifty-ninth Plymouth – remember?'

COLONEL: All these cars you gave away cost you well over a million dollars.

OLDER PRESLEY: Didn't miss one single cent. Brought a lot of happiness.

COLONEL: Ignoring the volleyball courts, for the time being, we've managed to get rid of two of the jet planes – but the other two still cost near two million – just to buy. Never mind the maintenance.

OLDER PRESLEY: Jesus Christ – do I have to pay maintenance to my goddamn aeroplanes as well as my wife?

86

VERNON PRESLEY: Son –

OLDER PRESLEY: I don't wanna talk about it.

COLONEL PARKER: Four months ago in Baton Rouge, you spent sixteen thousand two hundred dollars chartering a jet to bring you back a peanut butter sandwich.

OLDER PRESLEY: Didn't have my brand in Baton Rouge.

COLONEL: What was wrong with your own jets?

OLDER PRESLEY: I lent them to Tom Jones. His family were over from Wales.

(There is no point in talking to him this time. But . . .)

COLONEL: The truth is –

OLDER PRESLEY: Don't use that word. *(Turns to VERNON PRESLEY.)* The last time you made me cut down on expenses, Duke an' Gerry went – an' I'm gonna be payin' for that for the rest of my life.

VERNON PRESLEY: We'll put lawyers on it – they'll –

OLDER PRESLEY: But what happens if it's the truth?

COLONEL: *(Patience personified)* The facts are, Elvis, you keep on spendin' like this – you won't have any money left to spend. Goin' out faster than its comin' in – an' that's bad business. I think it's about time *you* started 'takin' care of business'.

(He stands, begins to quickly collect his accounts and papers. VERNON doesn't know whether to stay or go. COLONEL PARKER relights his broom-handle cigar.)

After all, you know where you came from, son – don't wanna go back there now, do you?

(He rests his hand casually but briefly on PRESLEY's shoulder. When he removes it, PRESLEY wipes his shoulder. COLONEL PARKER walks off. VERNON PRESLEY hovers.)

OLDER PRESLEY: *(To himself)* What is there left?

VERNON PRESLEY: *(Earnestly)* Just cut down on the gifts, son, sell a plane maybe, stop buyin' all them guns – or else shoot your jeweller.

(He laughs – alone and nervously.)

OLDER PRESLEY: *(Quietly)* No. *What is there left?* *(Turns towards VERNON.)* What else can happen? An' where's it gonna stop?

(*He holds his hand up, indicating he doesn't need nor want answering.*)

VERNON PRESLEY: It'll be all right, son.

(*He stands.* PRESLEY *looks up at him, disbelieving but silent.* VERNON PRESLEY *moves away, stops.*)

(*Plaintively*) Did remember your mama, you know, day before yesterday.

OLDER PRESLEY: (*Gently*) Well, that's where you an' I are different, daddy. (*Looks at him.*) Cos I've never forgotten her.

(PRESLEY *looks away, in dismissal.* VERNON PRESLEY *limps away, wounded again.*)

I wanna tell you somethin', Jesse, that daddy of ours does not understand the true significance of money. Did three years' hard labour for changing a fourteen-dollar food cheque to forty-four dollars. A lousy thirty bucks. And ever since then, he sweats every time he breaks a fifty . . . 'S all right – I'll leave you soon, Jess – gettin' late – but listen to this – an' you better be listenin', man, I'm Elvis Presley . . . (*Laughs quietly as he looks at the empty throne.*) Done it all. Done the lot. An' what've I got? What I end up doin'? Talkin' to an empty chair in an empty room . . . At three in the mornin'. (*Stands up.*) Move. (*Waits for a while, then looks away from the chair, as if Jesse has stood up. Then sits in Jesse's chair, points to his own chair.*) Sit there. Played two twins once, Jesse, you'd have loved that – identical twins – so what did they do – they gave me a blonde wig f' one of them! (*Waits further, stands up, hovers over his usual throne.*) Open your mouth wide and say 'Ahhh' (*Shakes his head.*) You're lucky to be alive, young man . . . (*The laughter is facing on him. Returns to and sits on Jesse's throne, facing his own.*) Come on, you bastard – *perform.* Come back with me, Jesse Presley. (*Sings:*) 'Oh why oh why can't my dreams come true . . . ?' Let me see you – I can see most everythin' I want to see – wanna see you now – right at the start, boy – you can do it, Jesse, cos you'd have had the one thing I never had . . . guess I never had the ability to . . . control my life. Wish I'd have been cleverer. I just ain't

. . . clever. Like that. Me – I could fail a blood test. But you an' me together, Jesse, my talent, my good looks, my sex appeal, my left leg . . . (*Perks up again.*) Ain't too much left for you. 'Cept for that one thing. You would have won. You would have won. You would have – I ain't complete without you, man. I done everythin' – 'cept win. Come on, you bitch of a boy, square the circle, Jesse . . .

(*Slowly a spotlight comes up on the* YOUNGER PRESLEY, *standing, guitar in hand – with everything and arrogance.*)

Oh yes. Yes yes yes. It's 'fifty-four, Jesse, you're 19 – I'm 19 – wanted to hear my voice on record, been thinkin' about doin' it for months, nervous about it, singin' behind closed doors – closet singer, Jesse – finally plucked up the courage – and, boy, did I mess up that first session – but you would have just gone straight up there to Sun Records, seen that lovely little lady, Miss Keisker, took hold of that prehistoric microphone, and you would have sang, boy!

(*The* YOUNGER PRESLEY *performs – the younger* JESSE PRESLEY *– in the recording studio, someone watching at the control-booth window above him, as he sings 'Trying To Get To You':*)

JESSE PRESLEY:

    I've been travelling over mountains,
    Even through the valleys too,
    I've been travellin' night and day,
    I've been running all the way,
    Baby, trying to get to you . . .
    Ever since I read your letter,
    Where you said you loved me too,
    I've been travelling night and day,
    I've been running all the way,
    Baby, trying to get to you.

    When I read your loving letter,
    Then my heart began to sing,
    Well, with many miles between us,
    But it didn't mean a thing,
    I just had to reach you, baby,

In spite of all that I've been through,
I kept travelling night and day,
I kept running all the way,
Baby trying to get to you.

Well, if I had to do it over,
That's exactly what I'd do,
I would travel night and day,
And I would still run all the way,
Baby, trying to get to you.

Well, there's nothing that could hold me,
Or keep me away from you,
When your loving letter told me,
That you really loved me true.
Lord above, He knows I love you,
It was He who brought me through,
When my way was dark and night,
He would shine His brightest light,
When I was trying to get to you!

(JESSE PRESLEY *finishes – no shyness or stammer. He looks towards the control-booth window.*)
You like that, Miss Keisker?

TANNOY VOICE: It was . . . fine, real fine.

JESSE PRESLEY: (*Easily*) That all? Sounded pretty sensational from down here.

TANNOY VOICE: (*Laughs.*) Listen, leave a contact when you go, would you?

JESSE PRESLEY: A what? Miss?

TANNOY VOICE: Somewhere we can get hold of you, Jesse.

JESSE PRESLEY: Oh yeah, sure. (*Walks away.*) You can get hold of me anywhere you want, Miss Keisker.

TANNOY VOICE: (*No edge*) That'll be all for now, thank you.

(JESSE PRESLEY *looks up, looks to the microphone, laughs, swaggers.*)

Gracelands. The viewing room.
The OLDER PRESLEY *– oh so happy.*
OLDER PRESLEY: Hey – hey! You're savin' my life! But I'd

have got that recordin' contract with Sun on my own, you
know – sorry, Jesse, but I would – come to think of it – I
did – but there's someone I want you to meet, man.
Someone who . . . who . . . ah, just meet him – tell me
what you would have done . . .

Colonel Parker's office.
JESSE PRESLEY *with* COLONEL PARKER, *at the colonel's desk.*
JESSE *has his feet on the desk, guitar in hand – James Dean time.*
He sings a slightly rewritten version of 'Treat Me Nice'.
JESSE PRESLEY:

> When I walk through that door,
> Brother, be polite,
> You're goin' to hurt me so
> If you don't greet me right,
> If you don't want me to be cold as ice,
> Treat me nice.
>
> I don't want to be your slave,
> Even if you ask me to,
> And if you don't behave,
> I'll walk right out on you,
> If you want my money, then take my advice,
> Treat me nice.

COLONEL: Well, Mr Presley –
JESSE PRESLEY: My friends call me 'Jesse'.
COLONEL: Ah. Erm right, Jesse –
JESSE PRESLEY: You can call me 'Mr Presley'.
COLONEL: About this contract, Mr Presley –
JESSE PRESLEY: Wanna ask you a question, Parker – what d'y'
    want? Fifteen per cent of millions or 50 per cent of fuck all?
COLONEL: That's a very easy question to answer, Mr Presley.
    (*He slides the contract across the desk, ripping up another one
    immediately afterwards – the 50 per cent one.* JESSE *teases him
    effortlessly.*)
JESSE PRESLEY: And when it comes time to go in the Army,
    man, open your wallet an' buy those boys off, understand?
COLONEL: Sure.

Gracelands. The viewing room.
The OLDER PRESLEY *is enjoying himself – and* JESSE. *He is standing on the table, as if trying to join in.*
OLDER PRESLEY: Hey no, wait! All right, don't wait – fast
    forward – *forward*. Wanna see what you would have done
    about Priscilla an' Mike Stone. You'd have sorted that out,
    Jesse – who knows, if it'd been you – or both of us together
    – hey, it wouldn't have needed sortin' – but just tell me –
    what would you have done?

A grotesquely graphic but fast scene of a MAFIA MAN *strangling*
MIKE STONE *horrendously with piano wire, his feet thrashing, while*
ANOTHER MAFIA MAN *stands happily behind them, inspecting his*
fingernails and whistling 'Don't Be Cruel'.

Gracelands. The viewing room.
The OLDER PRESLEY, *down on his knees, back turned, retreating*
fast. He stops, hands over his eyes. Turns back, peeps out.
OLDER PRESLEY: Jesus, man, *you would have done that?* (*Can't*
    cope with this, moves back to his chair, but tries to recover.)
    Better not tell me what you'd have done with Cilla . . .
    Could let me see how you'd have sorted out Duke an' Gerry
    though . . .

JESSE *takes a flick knife from his pocket, flicks it open, perhaps*
indicates to the TWO MAFIOSO MEN *with it. Then he carefully*
begins to clean his nails with the flick knife.

Gracelands. The viewing room.
OLDER PRESLEY: *Is that winnin'?* Is it? Is that how you win in
    this stinkin' world? Christ no, I don't want that, Jesse. Just
    make it happy, man. Happy. Give me . . . oh, I don't
    know, it's a lot to ask for, *but please give me some happiness*,
    let me keep my dignity. Please. Give me some peace of
    mind . . . some *tranquillity*. (*Stares out, sees her, lovingly,*
    before we do.) Oh . . . oh mama.
    (*A very old but still slim and pert and sweet* GLADYS
    PRESLEY *approaches* PRESLEY *at his table. Just like*

MARIE-ANNE. *She holds a tray of Good Ole Boys-down-home food. She places it in front of him. She moves away from the table, hobbling slightly – after all, she is in her seventies . . . The* OLDER PRESLEY *becomes more and more horrified and terrified by his night dreams.* GLADYS PRESLEY *moves away from the table, approaching (if we should be so lucky) a doorway.*)

GLADYS PRESLEY: (*Pleasantly, easily*) Jesse! Jesse! Don't know what you're doin' out there, but I ain' cookin' for the sake of it . . .

(*The* OLDER PRESLEY *approaches the scene. Cataclysmic. Trying to stop it, but terrified of touching it.*)

OLDER PRESLEY: No, no, no – mama! No mama – there's no Jesse there – only me – mama don't call him in. He ain't there, mama! (*Quietly*) My mama never made it to be a good old girl . . . Jesse never made it all. (*Stands up, shouts at the elements:*) Jesse, you gotta know – you were carried out at birth – second strike you went – Jesse, I want you to stop it now. Jesse . . . Jesse, Jesse, the only two people left to love me are my mama an' you . . . one is dead an' the other one never lived . . .

(*He begins to break down completely, hears the sound of funeral music, looks back. We hear 'All My Trials, Lord'.*)

PRINCIPAL SINGER:
    Hush little baby, don't you cry,
    You know your mamma was born to die,
    All my trials, Lord, soon be over . . .

(*A funeral cortège, a coffin being carried, approaching a grave. No other mourners – yet. The funeral cortège arrives. The* OLDER PRESLEY *believes it is his mother's funeral he is now witnessing. Then he sees a group of mourners approaching slowly:* VERNON PRESLEY, DUKE *and* GERRY, JO JO *and* MARTY, . . . *then* PRISCILLA – *and* REDHEAD *at a suitable remove. And he realizes as the coffin is lowered into the grave.*)

VERNON PRESLEY: Oh son, son son . . .

(*The* OLDER PRESLEY *falls to the ground – on his knees, his arms wrapped around himself, head hits the floor.*)

OLDER PRESLEY: No . . . no . . . no . . .

(COLONEL PARKER *arrives on the scene, dressed as a carnival con-man, wanders through the funeral cortège, carrying Presley memorabilia on a tray strapped around his shoulders – cheerfully. No one else notices him – except the* OLDER PRESLEY.)

COLONEL: Roll up, roll up.

OLDER PRESLEY: NO! NO!

(*He moves away from the funeral area towards the Gracelands area. The lights go down on the scene.*)

Gracelands. The viewing room.
The OLDER PRESLEY *is near to convulsion and total madness, hurtles at his throne, tries to hold the chair around himself, then falls off the chair.*

OLDER PRESLEY: No – no no no NO!

(JO JO *alone enters, ready to depart, jacket on, bags packed. Part of him wants to hide the bags or even go off, but the other bigger part wants to hold and pacify and love the man.* JO JO *throws the bags on the table, halfway there, and rushes towards the* OLDER PRESLEY *and comforts him. It is hard.*)

(*Finally*) I saw my mama, Jo Jo.

JO JO: It's all right, man, it's all right.

OLDER PRESLEY: Saw Jesse too.

JO JO: Just a bad dream.

OLDER PRESLEY: Jesse was alive, an' so was mama.

JO JO: It's –

OLDER PRESLEY: But I was dead.

JO JO: A nightmare, Elvis, an' it's all over now.

OLDER PRESLEY: I know. I was dead. I was.

JO JO: Don't let it –

OLDER PRESLEY: Saw it all, the past an' everythin' – saw the future – isn't one . . . no *no*!

JO JO: D'you want me to get you anythin'?

OLDER PRESLEY: Yeah, get me Reds, get her down here, I need her.

(JO JO *moves away from him, takes his jacket off, shakes his head, goes towards his bags, picks them up.*)

(*Little boy*) You goin' somewhere, Jo Jo?

JO JO: (*As he goes*) No, boss – goin' nowhere . . . washin', that's
all. Some . . . dirty linen.

OLDER PRESLEY: At a quarter to four?
(*He sits up in his chair, tries for calm. Breathes in deeply and
out, breathes in again. Hit by pain. And again. And again.
Goes to hold his chest. Doesn't get there. Falls to the floor.
Lights out on Gracelands.*)

A spotlight hits the YOUNGER PRESLEY. *He sings 'Are You
Lonesome Tonight?'*

YOUNGER PRESLEY:

> Are you lonesome tonight,
> Do you miss me tonight,
> Are you sorry we drifted apart,
> Does your memory stray
> To a bright summer's day,
> When I kissed you and called you sweetheart?
> Do the chairs in your parlour
> Seem empty and bare,
> Do you gaze at your doorstep and picture me there?
> Is your heart filled with pain,
> Shall I come back again,
> Tell me dear, are you lonesome tonight?

(*The light begins to go down on the* YOUNGER PRESLEY *as he
brings the song to an unexpected end.*)

TANNOY VOICE: Ladies and gentlemen, Elvis has left the
building.
(*Blackout.*)